# SCATTERED SIBLINGS
## An Adoptee's Search for His Biological Roots

**by**

**Lawrence A. Weeks**

laweeks6236@yahoo.com
http://scatteredsiblings.com/

Copyright 2006, 2013

INTRODUCTION

If you are not an adoptee or someone who has been looking for lost family members, you will probably find the emotional drive behind this story difficult to understand. But if you have been searching for your biological roots, you should be able to identify with the unexplainable drive that gnawed at me for years. This is a story about how one little piece of information led to another, and then another, and how there eventually seemed to be no end to the amount of doors to open and things to find out. Yet there also seemed to be no end to the amount of brick walls, dead ends, and stumbling blocks in my path. There are a lot of files with adoptees' names on them that are sitting in musty, dusty cabinets in stuffy buildings that are being deliberately kept from people who are looking for their roots.

The story of my search started in February of 1968, when I held my newly born daughter, Yvette, for the first time. Then one day, after my search had ground to a halt, there was an incredible coincidence in a small classroom in a large Cleveland college. My story continues to one sunny morning in July of 1996 on the top of a windy hill in a cemetery where I knelt in prayer at a long-forgotten grave. And yet again, I stumbled over another sibling's existence just when I thought my search was over.

I hope this story will inspire any adoptee or anyone searching for lost family members to never give up the search, to look around all corners, to be patient, and to use each piece of information with consideration for anyone who might be hurt by its being divulged. All the information that I uncovered was obtained without having to go to court. Nothing underhanded or sneaky was done to move from step to step in this story. Persistence, prayers, common sense, curiosity, and patience paid off.

Keep in mind that most orphans do not start as children of two well-situated parents who had no relatives, who were deeply in love, and who tragically died in a car crash. Very often people become orphans because of some reckless, irresponsible and, in some cases, almost unforgivable behavior of their parents many, many years ago. Unfortunately, not all searches have happy endings. In any case, say a prayer that you'll be successful, but be prepared for anything.

DEDICATED TO MY SCATTERED SIBLINGS:

Betty Jo (May she rest in peace)

JoAnn

Sally Ann Hayes

Terry Joe (May he rest in peace)

Norma Nell

and little Michael who will forever be six years old

# An Adoptee's Poem

*Once there were two women, who didn't know each other.*
*One you don't remember; the other you call mother.*

*Two different lives were shaped to make you one.*
*One became your guiding star; the other became your sun.*

*The first one gave you life; the other taught you to live it.*
*The first gave you a need for love; the second got to give it.*

*One gave you a nationality; the other gave you a name.*
*One gave you a talent; the other gave you aim.*

*One gave you emotions; the other calmed your fears.*
*One saw your first sweet smile; the other dried your tears.*

*One didn't have a home that she could provide.*
*The other's prayer for a child was not denied.*

*And now you ask me, through your little tears*
*The age old question, asked through the years:*

*"From that mom or this mom, which am I a product of?"*
*Neither, my Darling, neither. Just two kinds of love.*

Author Anonymous

**About the Book**

This is a story about an adoptee's search for his biological roots that lasted over 25 years. It relates how one little piece of information led to another, and then another, and how there eventually seemed to be no end to the amount of doors to open and things to find out. Yet there also seemed to be no end to the amount of brick walls, dead ends, and stumbling blocks in his path.

The story of his search started in February of 1968, when he held his newly born daughter for the first time. After his search had ground to a halt a couple years later, there was an incredible coincidence in a small classroom in a large Cleveland college. At one point, a number of newly found cousins, aunts and uncles swore that they had seen pictures of him dead and in a coffin. The story continues to one sunny morning in July of 1996 on the top of a windy hill in a cemetery where he knelt in prayer at a long-forgotten grave.

This story will inspire any adoptee or anyone searching for lost family members to never give up, to look around all corners, to be patient, and to use each piece of information with consideration for anyone who might be hurt by its being divulged. All the information that he uncovered was obtained without having to go to court. Persistence, prayers, common sense, curiosity, and patience paid off.

## My Search Begins

I drove my little green '94 Hyundai up to a guard shack at the front of the Columbia Trailer Park in Olmsted Township, Ohio. I had a large envelope on the front passenger seat containing various pictures of my family. On the rear floor of my car, propped up behind the front seat, I had a newly purchased planter wrapped in green florist's paper. And I also had a big smile on my face. I pulled my car up to the guard shack and rolled down my window.

"Yes?" questioned a little old lady.

"I'm here to see Elaine Lewis," I answered boldly.

"What's her address?" the lady asked, checking to see if I really knew anyone in the park.

I answered, "37 Elgin Oval."

After briefly looking over her list of residents, she nodded her approval and gave me permission to enter. This time I confidently used Elaine's name when the lady asked; the last time I was here, I had to make up a story about why I wanted to go into the trailer park. This time my birth mother, Elaine Lewis, was waiting to see me for the first time. After 50 years of separation, 26 years of searching, and just 44 miles of distance from my home, my birth mother and I were about to meet each other for the first time..

When I was about five years old, my parents told me I was adopted. At that age, the term adoption didn't mean too much to me. They told me that my parents died in a car crash when I was an infant and that I was then put in an orphanage where I was taken care of by nuns until my new parents came to take me home.

They told me that the name I was given when I born was *Joseph Allan Vincent*. So I had two names: *Joseph Allan Vincent* and *Lawrence Andrew Weeks*. I liked the name *Larry;* I didn't feel like a *Joseph*. I don't remember being told more than once that my name was *Joseph Allan Vincent*, but I never forgot it. And as you'll see, it was the main key to the beginning of my search.

According to Cleveland Catholic Charities records, I was born 5:10 p.m., Thursday, June 15, 1944, at St. Ann's hospital in eastern Cleveland. No abnormalities were reported. I was put in the St. Vincent DePaul Home until the time of my placement with my adoptive family.[1]

At the time of my birth, the adoption system consisted of matching children with families based on heritage and appearance. Their records suggest that I was difficult to place "due to coloring (orangish red hair and dark complexion)[2], and nationality/background[3], as well as personality." I had no idea

---

[1] information from *Background Information:* Prepared for Larry Weeks, Catholic Charities Service letter, August 9, 2000.
[2] (?) I am fair skinned with freckles.
[3] more on this later

what "nationality/background" meant; my new parents told me that I was "French and Central European." My personality was described as "fearful and sensitive." They said I had frequent temper tantrums and reportedly had difficulty relating to people[4]

On March 7, 1946, when I was then 23 months old, I was scheduled to have joined my adoptive family; but I was sick with a cold and placement was postponed. Then on March 24, 1946, I was brought on a bus to Euclid, an eastern suburb of Cleveland, to live on Ball Avenue with my new family that consisted of a mother, a father, and a 4½ year-old brother Michael (who was likewise adopted, but out of Lorain, Ohio). There were also two cats: an ornery tiger cat named Weenie (who liked no one but my new mother) and loveable, patchy-colored Pinkie (an adopted stray cat who had a lanced ear that lay flat on its head).

That first day in Euclid was a difficult one for me because I didn't want to leave the security of St. Ann's and the Sisters. They said I was fearful of the car, probably because I had never ridden in one before. After meeting my new family and looking around my new home, I settled down and seemed more relaxed; but I was supposedly somewhat apprehensive.[5]

In a letter from my adoptive mother to the agency, she reported that it had taken me a few days to get accustomed to the novelty of my new home and family, but that I had adjusted nicely. She stated that I

---

[4] information from *Background Information:* Prepared for Larry Weeks, Catholic Charities Service letter, August 9, 2000.
[5] Ibid.

was laughing and jabbering all day and would sing myself to sleep.

In May of 1946, an agency caseworker visited my new home and stated that she was amazed at the change in me. She stated that I had always been so solemn, had seldom smiled, and had never laughed; but now I was "laughing aloud, smiling frequently, and seemed very happy and contented." She said that I was still "bumping" my head, but much less frequently than when I first came. I was supposed to have frequently gotten on all fours in my crib and would rock back and forth while banging my head on the crib. My new mother reported that one night I had gone through the night with no "head bumping" at all.

Now, my new mother wrote, I was starting to say "button shoe," "bye-bye," "grandpa," "book," "momma," and "dada." My new mother said that my language development had picked up remarkably. She also added that since being on a schedule, I seemed to have become more at home; and my desire to be eating all the time disappeared, so I was eating only normal amounts for a growing child.

In March of 1947, an agency caseworker visited again and said I was talking very well; and I was occupying the majority of my time working with colored marbles and coloring books, was able to name my basic colors, and enjoyed listening to music. On September 8, 1947, my adoption officially went through, whereupon they immediately changed my first name to *Lawrenc*e (my new mother's father's first name, *Lawrence* Pozzi) and my middle name to *Andrew* (after the first name of my adoptive mother's best friend's father, *Andrew* Olsen).

My older adoptive brother, Michael Joseph, was also told that his parents died in a car crash. My younger adoptive sister, Madonna Ann, adopted two years after I was, likewise was told that her parents died in a car crash. It sure seemed like a lot of car crashes. We kids were each told of these fatal car crashes at different times and not within earshot of each other.

My brother was told he was Italian and Polish. I was told I was French and Central European (I never did find out what Central European meant, but that's what I was told whenever I asked about my nationality). My sister was told she was Irish and Polish.

My new mother was pure Italian. My new dad was German. We had a real "United Nations" house. Michael had black hair; but since my sister and I had the same auburn-colored hair, most people assumed that she and I were biological brother and sister, even though my eyes are brown and hers are green.

The term *adoption* didn't mean much to me. Being only five or six years old, I assumed that all babies were put in hospitals by God and were then picked up by parents whenever they wanted a baby. Our Catholic grade school primers showed a mom and pop on their way to the local hospital. The mother in the story was not graphically portrayed with any sign of a baby-belly; however, Mom and Pop would, in the next chapter, return home with a precious baby; and all was well.

Adopted kids, according to my line of reasoning, had been picked up by a family from a hospital (where God put them) but were then returned for some reason. So, I reasoned, following my original parents' fatal car crash, that I was brought back to the hospital after the funeral and was then available for someone else. Other than that, the concept of adoption didn't mean a thing to me.

## My New Surroundings

My new home was a two-and-a-half-story, wood frame house on Ball Avenue. Each house on the street had a driveway and a small strip of grass separating it from the next house. Each house had a small front yard and small back yard.

Our house had a big living room, a good-size dining room, a big front porch, and a small kitchen on the first floor. Upstairs were three bedrooms of modest size and a large bathroom. Stairs on the second floor led up to an attic that wasn't insulated until the year that my parents decided to put my brother Michael and me up there for our bedrooms once the second floor became too crowded. The attic was always terribly hot in the summer and very cold in the winter; and even after my parents nailed long strips of Kimberly Clark insulation into the internal beams of the sloped roof, it was still most uncomfortable. But Mike and I got used to the sleeping quarters and made the attic our personal room.

We had a full basement that included an old wringer washer, two wash tubs, lots of playing area, and lots of clothes lines strung from north to south on the basement's west side that were used to hang the wash in the winter months and inclement weather.

We three children made the south side of the large basement our main play area and had peach baskets full of our various toys. There always seemed to be food on the table, clothes on our backs, and a little bit left over for a movie, a trip or two to the local *Rollerdrome* for roller skating, or for ice cream cones.

Our street was full of kids of all ages and full of stay-at-home moms. Most families had only one car, and that car was with the father wherever he worked. Monday really was washday, and Thursday seemed to be food-shopping day. On Sundays you could scarcely find a gas station open, much less a corner food store. The kids could be found either in the street playing baseball, or in garages playing on various riding toys, or putting together puppet shows, or playing cops and robbers, or perhaps cowboys and Indians.

My new father, Warren Benjamin Weeks, who had been born in Milwaukee, Wisconsin, in January of 1907, met my mother in Illinois and was transferred to the Cleveland area by the Dr. Scholl foot people in the late 1930s or early 1940s. His father, Warren Edward Weeks, was a well-to-do banker in Davenport, Iowa; it is said that a nanny raised my father and my dad's only sibling, Evelyn, in rather opulent surroundings.

Following the stock market crash of 1929 and the subsequent collapse of my grandfather's bank, my father dropped out of the Colorado School of Mining to go home to help with his family's finances. Supposedly, my new grandfather paid back every penny that his investors had lost.

My adoptive father was not a tall man, maybe five foot seven or so; but he was very strong and had big biceps. I remember as a little kid sitting in his lap trying to put both my hands around his flexed bicep, which I could never quite do. He told me he played college football and basketball. He was a very loveable man who, following any spanking or punishment, would later try to get us to smile. I remember fondly sitting in his lap while messing up his hair as much as I could. Then he'd take out his comb, make a couple swipes, and it was all in place again.

My adoptive mother, Caroline Margaret Pozzi, was from Rockford, Illinois. She was the elder of two daughters of Italian immigrants, Lorenzo and Carolina Pozzi. She was a straight-A student throughout grade school, high school, and during her time at a two-year teachers' college.

Following college, Caroline worked as a clothing buyer at Hess Brothers in Chicago. She'd frequently get on the old passenger prop planes (which were new back then) and head to New York City to the fashion shows to order inventory.

Caroline's mother died at a young age of a stroke; and since Caroline's sister Marie was minor child ten years younger than she was, Caroline had to fill in as mother. It was always apparent to me that my mother was closer to her mother than her father; and for many years, she would have a Catholic Mass said every April 18 on the anniversary of her mother's birthday.

My adoptive mother was not an outwardly warm person, seldom showing physical affection. She also seemed to sorely lack the sense of humor and quick wit that my father had. And frequently I wondered as a child how two totally opposite people, such as they, had ever gotten together. She seldom laughed nor cried, but she was quick to show anger.

She exuded a rather regal air about herself to our neighbors. One neighbor told me that he could never refer to her as "Caroline." To him, she was always "Mrs. Weeks." And she seldom if ever visited neighbors who were outside in their yards; more often than not, they'd come over to our yard to visit her instead. I can't remember her sitting in anyone's yard or on anyone's porch. However, she was always the one to whom they'd turn for advice.

She was a devout Catholic and made my father convert to Catholicism before they were married; both of them were now in their late thirties. Although my mother had never been married before she met my father, I discovered in 2004, while doing census searching on the Internet, that my father had been married once before to a Swedish lady while living in Milwaukee, Wisconsin. There was no mention of any children. Up until 2004, neither I, nor my sister Madonna, nor my brother Michael had known anything about my father's previous marriage. I've wondered if my adoptive mother Caroline knew.

Soon after Warren and Caroline came to Cleveland, he worked briefly for Lincoln Electric in Euclid and then sold televisions and radios at The May Company in downtown Cleveland. Before long, he was selling furniture on May Company's sixth floor before being transferred to what used to be called May's-on-the-Heights.

Our family went to St. Christine's Catholic Church in Euclid, and the three of us children went to the old wood frame school that was part of the same church building. We had nuns of St. Francis of Christ the King who lived across the street from the school in "the old Schneider place," a home that looked more like an abandoned mom-and-pop store. For a couple years, when the main school became too crowded, some classes were taught in the nun's garage. If I remember right, my brother was across the street in that garage for his entire sixth grade.

For the most part, I have very pleasant memories of the hard-working nuns. They seemed to all be well-educated and very patient. Our eighth-grade nun, Sister Raphael, for instance, had fifty-five children in one room for the entire school year; apparently, she was unaware that she had "too many" children as we now hear from our modern teachers. Imagine a student-teacher ratio of 55:1 in one room and eighth graders to boot. We were all seated alphabetically, everything was orderly, we graded each other's papers in class, and sent our work to the front so they perfectly matched Sister's grade book.

Any miscreants (and we had a couple in the 8th grade, if my memory serves me) were dealt with by Fr. Tomc, the assistant pastor, who had a vise-like finger grip he'd use into the shoulder blades of anyone stepping out of line. Every six weeks, the good father would visit our classroom, sit in front of the room, and read our report cards aloud while he had brief discourses with each of us. "I see you went down in arithmetic, Johnny. What happened?" he might ask. And we'd all listen for Johnny's reply. Since I was a pretty good student in my beginning years, I don't remember having been put on the spot by Fr. Tomc.

We had an old pastor, Fr. Anthony Bombach, who had founded the Slovenian parish in 1925. I personally don't remember it, but my parents told me that when they moved to Euclid in the mid-1940s, there was a Slovenian Mass said every Sunday. And in my early teen years, I had a Slovenian paper route called *Enokoprovnost* (or something like that) that was scattered all over central Euclid.

On All Souls' Day, we Catholic kids were told that we could pray for the souls in Purgatory to help them be released into heaven. Purgatory was, after all, a holding area for those whose souls were not quite ready for heaven. I remember for many years praying fervently each year for my biological parents' release from Purgatory just in case they were still there. What better gift to receive from their orphaned son down on earth than a Purgatorial release into Heaven!

I didn't have too much reason to doubt the car crash story. It seemed plausible I guessed. One day I met a kid in school who was likewise adopted, and he had the same story about his parents' deaths in a car crash. It seemed odd to me that there were all those car crashes back then that left all those orphans. But there was no reason to doubt my parents. After all, my parents wouldn't lie about that, would they?

Once a year, for a few years, my parents would visit Parmadale, an orphanage on Cleveland's south west side where my sister and I would have resided had we not been adopted. There was a dear, sweet nun, Sister Xavier,[6] whom we would always meet there. She had taken care of Donna and me when we were in the infant orphanage at the St. Vincent DePaul Home. I still have a small scar on my lower lip that I got when I was running around the orphans' nursery with a drinking glass. Before the nun's were able to catch up to me, I fell, the glass shattered, and somehow I cut my lip. A couple stitches later, and I was as good as new.

At Parmadale, in neat little ivy-covered, brick cottages, were orphans being raised by the dear nuns. One age group to each home was the rule. When the kids were 18 years old and were armed with a high school diploma, they were put into the world to be on their own. It never dawned on me that these visits from us were probably not too easy for the kids in the cottages; after all, I could go home to a family— they had no family of their own. I wondered what they thought.

---

[6] Sr. Xavier: A dear friend of mine, Rachel Walker, read this manuscript in 2011, recognized the name Sr. Xavier, and found that the sister, in her early 90s, was still alive and well, living in a religious senior citizens' home in Richfield, Ohio. My sister Donna and I then visited her and brought pictures that were taken on these early Parmadale visits.

## The Birth Certificate

It was early February of 1968. I was approaching twenty-four years of age. It was in the middle of a snowstorm. My wife had just been released from the hospital after the birth of our first child, a 9-pound 4-ounce girl with curly red hair—a big baby. I sat in the car while my wife went into *Revco* drug store to get some *Similac®*. I held Yvette Suzanne for the first time. Here, buried in a fuzzy blanket, was a chubby bundle of pink skin, perfect little eyebrows, perfect little finger nails, and perfect everything.

I wondered if my biological parents in heaven were watching. Here was my first child, perhaps their first grandchild. Wasn't she perfect! But as far as a family tree went down here on earth, I was the trunk. I didn't know if I had any natural brothers or sisters who were scattered because of that awful car crash years ago. I knew nothing about my physical ancestors. Why was Yvette so big? What characteristics did my daughter get that were from that family that was broken up years before by that tragic accident?

Why, heck, I didn't even have a birth certificate. My parents got me into grade school, high school, and even into the Army by showing some kind of form that proved I was born in June of 1944; but it was not a birth certificate. Since I was starting my new family, I thought that I would like to get a birth certificate for the first time in my life.

My first letter to the Ohio Department of Vital Statistics was answered quickly; there was *NO* birth certificate on file for anyone named *Lawrence Andrew Weeks*. But how could that be? I was born in Ohio on June 15, 1944, wasn't I? I wrote asking that they look again. Again, nothing. "Well look," I thought. "If you can't prove I'm alive, then I'll stop paying taxes and stop crossing the street only on green." After all, Ohio is saying that apparently I do not exist. It made no sense.

Well, what if they were to try to look for a birth certificate with my birth name, *Joseph Allan Vincent*? That's the name my parents told me that I was born with years ago. Nah! Probably wouldn't work, but it was worth a shot.

What came back in the mail a week later triggered a search that lasted from my mid-twenties until I was fifty years old (and beyond, I might add). I received a birth certificate for someone named *Joseph Allan Vincent*. This person, *Joseph Allan Vincent*, was the same person that I was. And there on the right side of the certificate was *Joseph's* mother's name: *Elaine Vincent*.

I was in awe. Right there in front of my eyes, the beginning of a story was unfolding—my story. I felt like I was eavesdropping in a stranger's life, but it was my natural mother's life and, therefore, my life—our lives. Elaine was 22 years old at my birth. She was from St. Paul, Minnesota. She was a press operator. She lived at 3115 Chatham Avenue in Cleveland. I was 8 pounds 6 ounces. I was full term.

Who was my *father?* I stared at the blank lines on the left side of the certificate under "Father." All it said was "Unknown." Therefore, Elaine Vincent, the lady on my birth certificate, was not married when I was born; and, apparently, she didn't know my father's name. Or, if she did know, she didn't want it on the certificate. Or maybe Elaine knew who he was and married him shortly after I was born; and *then* they died in a car crash. But if she knew who he was when I was born, then why didn't she put my father's name on the certificate? And if she didn't know who he was, then what kind of a person was she? But she must have known, because I was told that they both died in a car crash. And on and on I mentally rambled.

The birth certificate I was looking at was made three years *after* I was born—a year after my adoption; but my original name still hadn't been changed to my new name. Maybe they forgot to transfer that information to a rewritten certificate. Maybe she didn't want it on the certificate. Oh well, maybe that was not something you did way back then. And if she did marry my father, then why was my last name the same as hers? Wouldn't her last name change when she got married?

My curiosity wouldn't let this die. I had to know more. And as I found out, hardly anything I learned in the next 26 years would be smooth and uncomplicated; one newly opened door would lead to another closed door. My search had barely started.

## The Trip To The Library

A few months after my daughter Yvette's birth in 1968 (when I was 24 years old), and armed with my "new" birth certificate, I took a day off work and went to the Cleveland Public Library. I was going to spend a day seeing what I could find. After entering the big, massive building on Cleveland's Superior Avenue, I was directed to the second floor History Department. After going down a long hallway, I turned into a room with thousands of books, some on the many shelves on the first level, and thousands more up on a mezzanine level.

"Do you have old phone books from 1944?" I asked a sweet old lady at the reference desk.

"Certainly," I was told. "What do you need from the book?"

"Well, I'm trying to find a lady who lived in Cleveland in 1944."

"It's going to be hard to find a woman's name in a phone book, particularly in 1944," she offered. And the librarian was right. "How about a city directory?" she offered.

"What's a city directory?"

"It's in three parts: It lists everybody alphabetically by name, address, and phone number; and then everybody gets listed by street address, name and phone number; and then by phone, name, and address." My head was spinning trying to imagine what she was saying. "They're used by advertising companies and salesmen," I was told. It seemed confusing, but what the heck; it was worth a try.

She pulled out the big 1943-44 Cleveland City Directory and looked for *Elaine Vincent.* And there it was. The address listed for Elaine Vincent was the same as the one on my birth certificate; and it also listed the name of the company, *HPL Manufacturing, Co.*, where she was a press operator. My birthmother's occupation agreed with the birth certificate's information, and now I knew where she worked!

I was impressed. I was fascinated. Information on an old birth certificate that seemed so abstract at first was now staring at me in a public reference book. This made Elaine and the birth certificate all the more real. I was on my way.

When I looked through the part of the directory that was sorted by street names and addresses, the directory showed that Elaine's address was really a four-unit apartment; but none of the listed tenants had her last name. Perhaps she roomed with one of those families. Perhaps she lived with the parents of the person who was my birthfather. Perhaps they took care of her while she was pregnant. That would have been generous, I thought. She came from St. Paul, Minnesota, got pregnant, and lived with my father's family, then married my father, and then died in a car crash.

I went to the musty-dusty shelf where the librarian had gotten the 1943-44 city directory, couldn't find one for 1945 or 1946, but found the 1947 city directory and brought it to where I had all my paperwork. Let's see what's in this directory. But, Elaine was *not* in the 1947 directory. Maybe she died (as I was told by my parents), or perhaps she moved. She wasn't in the 1949 directory either, so possibly she really, really did die (after, of course, she had married my father, right?); and then they died in a car crash. Why would my adoptive parents mislead me? Let's look in one more directory.

I opened the 1951 city directory and was shocked. There she was. If this was the same *Elaine Vincent*, then she was alive in 1951 when I was six years old . . . a year or so *after* I was told that she died in a car crash. She was still apparently single and a press operator now working for a different company, *Langenau Manufacturing*, a small stamping company on Cleveland's near west side.

She was listed as living with a family not far from the factory. A trip through the next chronological city directories showed Elaine to have lived with yet another family, again, still close to the factory, and showed that she got promoted at *Langenau Manufacturing* from being a press operator to being a receptionist. She was still listed, though, as single and as living with the second of the two families with whom she had roomed.

The 1963 Cleveland city directory was her last appearance. In that directory, she was listed as living on Cleveland's west side in Bay Village, Ohio, and still working at *Langenau Manufacturing* as a receptionist. Then the trail went cold. She did not appear in any of the remaining city directories after 1963. So I concluded that she had either died, had moved, or had gotten married.

But most important, it showed that just five or so years before I was standing there (1968) looking at the 1963 city directory, Elaine was alive. She was alive when I was 19 years old. She was alive when I went to grade school. She was alive when I graduated from high school. She was alive when I got out of the Army. Maybe she was alive when I got married in 1966. Maybe she's alive right now! She had not died in a car crash. I was in awe. And if my calculations were correct and, if she were still alive, Elaine would be about 46 years old, a relatively young lady.

What did she look like? Where was she? Who was she? Was she tall, short, fat, or skinny? Maybe I passed her on a crowded street in Cleveland? Maybe I sat next to her at a ball game? Had I spoken to her while standing in a line somewhere? Did she look like me? I had auburn hair. Did she? I had fair skin and freckles. Did she?

But where did Elaine go? What happened to her after 1963? All I had was the name of the last company where she worked. Looking in the current Cleveland phone book didn't help; there were no *Elaine Vincent*s in the phone book. I could go downtown again to see if a person by her name died or got married during or after 1963. So, I went back to the Cleveland City Hall and searched. More dead ends. No such person got married in Cleveland, nor did anyone by that name die.

Back I went a couple blocks away to the Cleveland Public Library. City hall to the library–library to the city hall–then back to the library. I was beginning to wear a path between the two buildings. Do you have obituaries? Yes. How far back? The clerk told me that she could go back to 1850. I didn't need to go back that far. How about the past five years? I got introduced to microfilm and the fun you have trying to keep the rolls from jumping off the reel holder when you fast-forward or rewind. There is no sound on earth like the rapidy-flap-flap of the end of the microfilm strip slapping against the rollers; and you get to see what the people around you look like as they turn to face you with their nasty looks.

My search ground to a halt. I couldn't think of anywhere else to go. I could call all the *Vincent*s in the phone book to see if they knew her, but then I might accidentally bump into her on the phone. I was not ready for that. What if I accidentally contacted a brother or uncle? My adoptive mother, Caroline, was still alive and would very definitely not like me pursuing such a search. My adoptive father, Warren, had died in 1965, so I couldn't imagine what he would have thought.

Whatever I did had to be quiet, secretive, and well thought out. Neither my adoptive brother nor sister expressed any desire to know anything about their biological parents. And here I was plodding through very delicate and sensitive fields of information. But, nevertheless, other than contacting the last company that Elaine worked for to see if she was there, I could think of no other avenue to explore. But the intrigue and the unfolding mystery was a huge magnet. I couldn't stop. I was beginning to be excited about the whole thing.

## One Day In College

After my divorce in 1970 from Yvette's mother, I kept custody of Yvette and remarried in 1977 to Renee, a recent divorcee who also had custody of her two-year-old daughter Leslie. I started going to Cleveland State University in 1973 in the evenings pursuing a degree in history. Even though I had graduated from Euclid High School in 1961, I had not finished college. I took a psychology course in the Army through American University and had taken a few Kent State Extension courses at Euclid High School in the evenings, but I had never seriously put forward the effort to get a degree. But, knowing that I was a pretty smart guy (wasn't I?) and proving I was a pretty smart guy were two different things; I decided to go to night school and get a degree in something—anything.

Because I worked full time during the day, I became a "half-time" student at night. Therefore, what would normally take four years to accomplish would need twice the time to finish. I was in no rush though. My job in inventory control had nothing to do with teaching, but it paid the bills; and the company I was working for was paying for part of my tuition. Originally I had a desire to major in psychology in order to teach high school; but for some reason, I was getting very good grades in history and anthropology courses. And, after some soul searching, I decided to stick with history, mostly concentrating on American history.

One evening about five or six years after my search for my birthmother had ground to a halt, I arrived at a Cleveland State history class 15 minutes early. I sat in my usual desk, and there in front of me was a young man with whom I had chatted over the past few weeks before each class. I didn't know his name, and he didn't know mine; but we usually exchanged pleasantries before each class.

Before class while he sat in front of me, he turned to his left, sat sideways, and started some small talk. He took out his wallet while we were talking, pulled out some of the contents, sorted a few things, and then put them back into the wallet. He had a few business cards that he wanted to put elsewhere in his wallet, so he put them in a neat little stack on the upper left corner of my desk next to his left shoulder. We continued talking. It would be nice to know his name. I was too bashful to ask, so I casually glanced at the business cards stacked there in front of me. I saw his name—and then I saw the most unbelievable thing.

There on his business cards that were sitting on the corner of my desk was not only his name but also the exact name of the company that Elaine Vincent worked at in 1963 in her last available listing in the city directory. I looked with amazement and pointed to the name *Langenau Manufacturing Co.*

"Is that where you work?" I asked.

"Yeah. I've been a purchasing agent there for a while." He told me the company was not a large company and had only a few people in the office and a small bunch in the factory.

My God! This was too much of a coincidence!

"Omigod! I need your help," I said staring at him in disbelief. "Do you know anyone at work whose name is *Elaine*?"

"No."

"Are there any old timers there who might know of any Elaine?"

The young man said that there were a few people in the office who had been there awhile. "Why do you want to know?" he asked.

I told him of my search for my birthmother and how my search had run out of gas a few years earlier. The last information I had on her was the fact that she worked at *Langenau Manufacturing* in 1963.

"Would you be willing to ask someone about her?"

"Sure," he said.

"Please, whatever you do," I cautioned, "the information has to be very carefully gotten. I would rather not have her contacted."

He promised that he would do what he could and would get back to me before our next class. I gave him my name and phone number in case he needed it, and then I very nervously waited.

I made sure I was in class earlier than usual the following class day. Five minutes before class, the young man came in, sat down, and looked at me nervously. "I gotta' see you after class. It's important," he said.

"What happened?" My back went cold.

He looked at me directly and said, "Your mother is alive and well, lives by the airport, and denies you exist."

"What? You contacted her?" I said in disbelief.

"Well," the young man said, "the first person I asked when I went into work had worked with Elaine for years at *Langenau* and was shocked. Since she never heard of Elaine's having any children, the lady went to the owner of the company, a lawyer, and who also had known her, and told him of my conversation. They were both shocked and didn't know what your motives were, so they called her!"

"They called her? Why?" I was both angry and scared. I hadn't wanted them to go that far.

The young man looked at me and answered, "They figured that she should be told that someone is claiming to be her child."

"Oh my God!" I felt my back go cold. "She denied having a child?"

"Yeah, she denied that you exist," he continued, "and said that her sister-in-law or somebody is trying to start trouble."

I sat there shaking. Wow! "Then she MUST be my birthmother," I suggested.

"But she said she wasn't your mother," he said.

"Think about it," I reasoned. "If the situation weren't true at all, she'd want to know what you guys were talking about. She wouldn't have gotten mad. She just might have thought whoever said she had a kid was nuts."

"I don't get it," he said while looking puzzled.

"Don't you see? She got angry, denied I existed, and then cut off the conversation. That's the clincher—her instant denial."

For the first time in our two lives, my birth-mother knew I was alive, and I knew she was alive. In a rather bizarre way, we had made our first contact! I didn't think *Hallmark* had a card for such an occasion, but we had made our first contact with each other.

I asked if I could speak to the person who knew her. "Do you think Elaine's friend would mind if I called to ask a few questions?"

"No. Not at all. In fact, she asked me to tell you to call her." He gave me the name of the lady to whom he had spoken and told me that he found all this extremely fascinating. He told me that he hoped there would be a happy ending. So did I.

I drove home that night from college with my mind racing and a cautious smile on my face. My mother knows I'm alive; I know my mother's alive. She knows she's been found. Always having been a very apprehensive and cautious guy, I started to think of how she could retaliate against me: a lawsuit, a court drama where my adoptive family would find out and disown me, something or other that would hurt my family financially, and on and on my mind raced.

Then I'd go back to thinking how nice it was to know that she now knew that her son was aware that she was alive. And how nice it was that she had reacted and stirred because of something I did whether or not I wanted it to happen.

I couldn't wait to tell my wife about the news, which I considered to be good news; but then again, maybe it was bad news. If I ever needed to pray, it was now. "The toothpaste was out of the proverbial tube."

## The Clincher

The next day I called the lady with whom the young man had spoken. Delores was the personnel manager and therefore knew many employees from the past. She seemed very nice and was open to discuss what I had brought to light.

"I've known Elaine and Jimmy, her late husband, for years. I socialized with her, went to their house at Christmas time, and exchanged gifts; and she never, not even once, ever hinted that she had had a child. But," she said, "there was always something about her that I couldn't put my finger on. Something that made me think that there was something she was hiding. She was always very critical of women in the office who dressed provocatively—very judgmental. Anyway, what makes you think that she's your mother?"

"Well," I answered trying to hold the phone while looking at my birth certificate, "the Elaine Vincent person on my birth certificate was 22 years old when I was born." I told Delores my age and added 22 years.

"Well, that's the correct age," she acknowledged. "But what else?"

"And, my birth certificate says she came from St. Paul, Minnesota."

"Well, yes that's true, but so what else?"

"It says she was a press operator during the year I was born, and the city directory for 1951 said she was still a press operator and eventually worked her way up to being a receptionist at your company."

"Anything else?" Delores asked.

I was incredulous. I'd thought that these multiple "coincidences" would be proof enough; I didn't have anything else to offer. "That's not enough?" I asked.

"What's your nationality?" she asked.

"Well, I was told that I was French and Central-European."

"Sorry," Delores offered. "The French part is OK, but Elaine is also part American Indian."

*"Indian?"* I was startled.

"And she's proud of it," she continued.

*Indian?* Now, there's one I had never heard. I know I never would have forgotten had my parents told me that years ago.

"Well, I guess it's possible that I'm very wrong," I said. But there were too many coincidences, certainly; but the Indian part caught me off guard.

Not wanting to end the conversation since she had thrown cold water on my information, I asked her what Elaine looked like.

"Well, she's short, about 5 feet 2 inches. She has piercing blue eyes and light curly gray hair," she answered.

My eyes are brown, and my hair was auburn as a child. Well, since the Indian part was confusing to me, I told the lady that I would contact her if I came up with anything more convincing. She said she would be glad to help me if I had more information.

Now I was lost. If I went back to my adoptive mother and asked her about my being part Indian, I would tip my hand about searching for the unsearchable. Where would I go? I called the Catholic Charities in Cleveland, the agency from which I was adopted, and spoke to a social worker who specialized in handling adoptee inquiries.

All I wanted to know was anything, anything at all about my birth parents. What could she tell me? Could I see the records? After all, I was now an adult and didn't need protection. The information was about me—it was my information.

She was not impressed. "The records are closed. You'll have to go to court to get a release for such information." She would not budge. However, she added, she could review the file to see if there were any non-identifying bits of information that she could tell me. "Give me some time, and I'll get back to you," she promised.

A few weeks later, I got a call from the lady from the agency; she would like to see me. She had some information she had gathered that might be helpful. Please come down.

I drove to the old Woodland Avenue Catholic Charities building on Cleveland's near east side; and since I was told over the phone that this was where I was born, I began to wonder as I walked in. My birthmother might have walked these halls. She might have come through this door, or that door, or looked out this window, perhaps looking at the same street at which I was now looking. I was ushered by the receptionist into a small chapel in the center of the building and asked to wait for the lady to whom I'd spoken on the phone.

I looked around the little, quiet chapel and wondered if the baptismal font at the front of the church was the one used for my baptism back in 1944. The chapel was peaceful and very solemn. I felt my birthmother's presence from years ago. She might have knelt on one of these kneelers in one of these pews in front of one of these statues. She might have knelt in the pew where I was now. Then again, maybe this chapel was built later, much later. Who knew? I could hardly imagine what it was like in 1944 to show up here pregnant and unmarried.

The silence of my daydream was broken when suddenly, from the rear of the chapel, I heard the sharp, approaching stiff clicks of a woman's high heels. My name was called. "Mr. Weeks? Please follow me," a rather serious looking lady entreated.

We went down the hall and into a windowless, sparsely appointed room with a big table. She closed the large doors and motioned for me to sit in one of the big chairs. Her hair was dark and pulled back in a tight bun. The handsome woman was dressed in dark business attire. She put a thick manila folder down on the table, put her elbow on it, took off her dark rimmed glasses and began to discuss what information was available to me and what I'd have to do if I wanted more. She seemed polite and friendly, but I could just see in her eyes the reflections of many adoptees like me who had already gone before her stoic, frozen gaze to receive the same cautioning words.

I told her that I knew how delicate this situation was. I told her about the accidental contact with my birthmother that had been made by the people at Langenau Manufacturing and how upset I was that it had gone that far.

"Yes, I knew I was playing with fire," I told her. "But I didn't think the people I contacted would've gone as far as contacting her."

"Mr. Weeks, when she gave you up for adoption at birth, she was guaranteed to not have to worry about being contacted some day. Our records are shut at the moment that the adoption goes through."

"Well," I answered. "I'm not a little kid. If I were twelve years old and trying to get information about my natural family, it would be different. But I'm a grown man with a family, and you have information about me that you're telling me I'm not allowed to see. I admit that this situation went further than I'd wanted it to, but I still feel I did the right thing."

"I will be glad to be an intermediary if you ever do find your birthmother; I've done that before. My experience, though," she cautioned, "is that very few reunions are successful."

"But," I said, "I've seen on television that over 75 percent of reunions are successful."

"I'm not so sure about that," she said. "It's a dangerous area to pursue. See what happened in this case? You thought you could get close to her anonymously, but it backfired. Be cautious," she warned.

From inside the thick manila folder, she took out a № 10 business-sized white envelope and opened it. She handed me a sheet of paper folded into three parts. I began to read:

*The following is the only material available concerning background information for Lawrence Andrew Weeks, Birthdate 6/15/44.*

*<u>Biological Mother:</u> She was a single young woman in her early 20's. Her heritage was Roman Catholic, French-Canadian with a very slight trace of Indian...*

I stopped reading—my eyes were riveted on the word *Indian*. "Oh my God," I said to myself. "Indian!" I continued reading...

*...Her family origins were not in the State of Ohio. She was a high school graduate and was employed in factory work.*

*Brief reference to the maternal family makes note of the fact that there were several children but does not indicate where the mother ranked chronologically. There was some economic hardship with which she had difficulty coping.*

*<u>Biological Father:</u> He was not known to the Agency. He had been in Service and was described as being in his early 30's and was of*

*German heritage. It was stated that he had musical talent. He resided in his parental home.*

*These young people had met at an Army Camp. They have considered marriage but could not do so because of the fact that the biological father had been married previously.*

There it was . . . *"a very slight trace of Indian."* Bingo! I was part Indian. I struck oil. Now all I had to do was call Delores and tell her what I had found. And now I had information about my birthfather, too. *Musically inclined.* I had taught myself how to play chords on the guitar. Maybe that's where it came from.

I was angry, though, that I could see the thick manila folder under her elbow that contained information about me; but I was not allowed to see anything in it. She could put that folder in her briefcase, take it home, and leave it on a table for others in her house to see; but *I* could not see what was in there. That offended me. I politely thanked her for her time; and after a lukewarm handshake and receiving some more cautionary words from her, she sent me down the hall to the exit.

I found a phone in the lobby of the agency, fumbled for a dime, and called Delores at Elaine's former factory and eagerly read to her about the Indian ancestry. "Yep, I've got to see you," she said. "Can you come to my office now?"

I hopped in my car and headed for Cleveland's west side to search for the little factory on Madison

Avenue. My thoughts were racing as I drove over the Detroit Avenue Bridge. I drove down Madison Avenue, pulled into the factory's parking lot, parked in a visitor's spot, and paused.

From the street to the door at the center of the building was a narrow sidewalk. I looked at this walkway imagining my birthmother getting off a bus or a streetcar at the curb, walking up the same sidewalk, and then into the building. And how many times did she go up that walk, I wondered.

I walked up to the front door, slowly opened it, and stopped at the receptionist's window. I imagined my birthmother sitting at that very window and told the lady behind the desk that I had an appointment with the Human Resource director. Perhaps my birthmother used to sit at that same window, looking through the same glass years ago. Years ago.

I was ushered to an office down the hallway. As I walked in, a pleasant-looking, businesslike woman looked at me and exclaimed as I walked in, "You look just like her! You have her mouth!"

My head was spinning. I sat down, showed Delores the agency's letter, and waited for her response. She carefully read each word and then sat back and stared at me.

"I guess that clinches it," she concurred. "I guess you're right."

I felt very comfortable now as she began talking to me with a smile on her face.

"Your mother's been a widow since 1972 and had a radical mastectomy in the late 60s. Right now she lives alone in a house on the west side somewhere near the airport."

A small picture of Elaine started to emerge as I listened.

"I think a reunion with her would be perfect at this time," she said with a smile. "Elaine has no local family and no husband. She's all alone. I think it would be exciting for such a reunion?"

"I really don't think I'm ready for that," I said. "All I want to do is to get some information about her, anything that will not invade her privacy. And I still feel awful that her privacy had been invaded when you guys contacted her. If you wanted to know my motives, I wish you would have called me first."

She looked at me as though she didn't know what to say.

"Has Elaine contacted you since that call?" I asked.

"No. Elaine sounded very upset," she said.

When I told her how much information I'd gotten from the city directories, she was surprised. I told her that the directories showed me that Elaine had roomed with two families near Langenau Manufacturing before she disappeared from the book in 1963.

"Well," she said, "in 1963 she got married to a very nice man, the same man who died nine years later. And since I don't want to invade Elaine's privacy by giving you direct information, Larry, all I will say is that, at one of the homes she boarded, Elaine married the landlord's brother-in-law."

We talked for about an hour. I thanked Delores for her willingness to be as open about Elaine as she had been. "Please," I implored, "let's stay in contact." Maybe every so often, I said, I'd call her and ask her things about my birthmother. She said she'd be happy to stay in touch with me and told me to call her at work whenever I wanted.

Again she repeated that a reunion would be wonderful at this stage of Elaine's life. I agreed but told her that I was not ready to do so. I had hoped that I had not hurt her relationship with Elaine. And I had hoped that I had not ruined any chance to meet her someday.

I left the little factory with a lighter step. I had found a source of information whom I would contact over the next few years. And eventually, she'd be more help to me than she could ever imagine.

## Identifying Elaine

I went home feeling very happy after my meeting with Elaine's friend. At last I had a contact who seemed to believe my story. Since she had my phone number, I was sure she'd call me if anything happened to Elaine or if Elaine ever called her and wanted to meet me.

Ever since I met my second wife in 1976, I had shared my birth-parent searching drama with her. Reneé was afraid that I would hurt someone and wondered what would happen if my adoptive mother found out. I knew that neither my adoptive mother nor my adoptive sister would accept any of this. They both felt that one should "let sleeping dogs lie."

I digested the information that Elaine's friend had given me. I rolled it around in my mind as often as I could. I stared at the gathered bits and sheets of paper with my notes and scribblings. I did not know Elaine's new married last name. I did know, however, that she married the landlord's brother-in-law; but which landlord? Her friend Delores had told me about that. And I also knew that Elaine's husband died in 1972. Not much to go on. I let my search drop into another phase of inaction. What more could I do? But I'd nod off to sleep each night rolling this information over and over again in my mind.

One day, a year or two later, I suddenly had an idea pop into my mind. What if I could trace the names of the people with whom she lived to see what happened to them. And what if I could find an obituary (if they died, of course) for either of two landlords whose family she lived with? Let's see. If the head of the household died, his obituary will say *Schmoe, Joe, the beloved husband of Alice (nee XXXXX), blah, blah, blah*. The *nee* part would give me the deceased's wife's maiden name. And if Elaine married that widow's brother, then I'd have the last name of Elaine's husband. Then all I'd have to do is find someone with that last name who died in 1972 (the year Delores had told me) who was married to Elaine. Confusing? A needle in a haystack? Possibly. But there were only two haystacks—she roomed with only two families.

If either one or both of those men died, their obituaries would yield their wives' maiden names. The odds were small, but what the heck. I liked going to the library anyway; and what more fun could there be than loading up a noisy whippidy-whap-slapping, whiz-whirring microfilm machine and digging through musty-dusty books again?

Off I went. I checked the library's necrology department's obituary file and found that both of the men whose families Elaine lived with had died—bad news for them, I guessed; but good news for me. And each obituary listed the dead man's address (each obituary agreed with the addresses I had already uncovered) and listed the maiden name of his beloved wife. And guess what? Both widows had the same maiden last names . . . *Lewis*. They were most likely sisters . . . sisters of Elaine's late husband. Too easy, I thought.

So, all I had to do was find an obituary of a (*somebody*) *Lewis* who died in 1972 and whose obituary would list *beloved husband of Elaine (nee Vincent)*. What are the odds? How many *Lewises* were there who died in 1972? Not too many, I figured. I mounted the *L* obituary microfilm tape and within a few minutes—bingo—I had found the obituary of Elaine's late husband; and his name was listed as *James E*. I photocopied the obituary. So, now I had proof positive that Elaine's last name was (and is) *Lewis*. Quite a discovery, I thought. Bully for me!

There I searched city directories and old phone books for any *James Lewis* data. I found a few *Lewises* in 1972 and checked the previous year, but none of them listed Elaine as wife. Nor were there any listings in any year after that. Nor were there any listings for *Mrs. James E. Lewis* or *Mrs. Elaine Lewis*. So, although I had come quite far in just one visit to the library, I was back up against the proverbial brick wall again. James and Elaine must have undoubtedly kept their addresses and phone numbers unlisted.

There was no address in the *Plain Dealer* obituary from the library. Generally, there are no addresses listed in big-city newspapers obituaries. If I wanted to know more, then I would have to find a local community newspaper and hope they had a more extensive obituary article.

I contacted the *Sun Newspaper* chain in Cleveland and asked them what local paper was published in the Berea area. Soon I contacted the *Berea Sun Times*, asked them if they could dig back to 1972 and find an obituary for James Lewis. After a long pause, a young lady read me the local paper's obituary that had James Lewis's address, funeral home, place of work, and the cemetery where he was laid to rest.

Checking the address in the local newspaper's obituary led nowhere. There was no such address as the one listed. What I didn't know until years later was that I was looking in the wrong city for the street information. Part of the street on which Elaine lived in 1972 was in two different cities that were in two different counties.

I did, however, find a *James E. Lewis* in a nearby city whose wife's name was listed as *Margaret*. Since the home was very close to the deceased's home, I reasoned that this, in fact, was Elaine's new address. The name *Margaret*, perhaps, was her middle name; and perhaps she didn't use her first name. I rested a little comfortably thinking that I now knew where she was. All I had to do was call her up or write a letter to her whenever I wanted.

## A Dangerous Obsession

I've have difficulty explaining why I was so wrapped up in this search. Had I not been told that I had been adopted, I probably wouldn't have been any wiser. For many reasons, though, my relationship with my adoptive mother had always been strained. My adoptive parents married in their late 30s, rather late in life by the standards back then. In 1943, after being unable to have their own children, my new parents adopted my older brother Michael from an agency in Lorain, Ohio.

However, in 1944, the same year I was born, my adoptive mother had a full-term, stillborn baby. In later years I felt that perhaps some of my mother's feelings toward me had a lot to do with the fact that, although I was the same age as her lost son, I was not *THAT* son.

And the fact that she was in her late 40s and perhaps going through menopause probably didn't help either. In any case, I became a ready object of her approach to discipline, which was very rough and, at times, unchecked. Although my adoptive father was a kind and loving man, he generally stayed out of the way when her brand of discipline was dished out.

My problems consisted of untreated asthma, a misdiagnosed skin allergy to cats, frequent and heavy corporal punishment, facial and throat tics, and uncontrollable bedwetting that ran into my teens.

I became very unsure of myself, withdrawn, self-conscious, and very isolated. Other than my father's warm hugs, I had no other port of refuge. Many was the night that I'd go to sleep wondering why did they adopted me if I was this bad of a child.

So, I retreated into a world of daydreaming and comedy, turning most of my problems into humor, making light of bad situations, and being the guy you could turn to for a few laughs. My light-hearted approach to life belied a great deal of my internal struggle to get acceptance. It was hard for me to get serious about anything, a trait that I found useful in maintaining my sanity.

Once I was married and on my own, and especially following Yvette's birth, I became obsessed with putting together all those missing pieces. I had never heard my brother or sister showing any interest in such a search, but I was obsessed by it. What would they think of me if they knew? How far could I go? What would I do if I were to meet my birthmother?

When I remarried in 1977, my new wife, Renee; my daughter Yvette; Renee's daughter, Leslie, from her first marriage; and I lived in a townhouse in Mentor, Ohio, just east of Cleveland in a reconstructed nuclear family.

Since each townhouse unit was a rental, we frequently had new neighbors. In September of 1981, we got new neighbors from Pittsburgh, Pennsylvania. Joe and I would kid around about the Browns and Steelers, and we would taunt each other during the football season. Joe worked at a newspaper in Geauga County, a small county next to the one we lived in; it had a small paper with a rather modest number of readers.

One day, after I discussed my search for birthparent information, he told me that one of the writers on his small paper was doing a series on adoptees looking for birthparents. Would I mind if this gentleman contacted me for an interview? Of course, I wouldn't mind, but anonymity would be of the utmost concern. No problem.

The next evening, a reporter from his paper called me. I told him about my search and how I had found out that my birthmother was alive and living somewhere in the Cleveland area. I also told him that I couldn't tell my young daughter that she was part Indian because she might leak that to my adoptive sister and adoptive mother. My relationship with them wasn't good anyway, and news of a search of this nature would make it even worse. I insisted on anonymity. No problem about that, I was assured. He'd change my name and other details so it would not be specific.

One big concern I had was that someone who knew my adoptive mother might read such an article and put two and two together and call her. As long as my identity was buried under a few layers of editing and a name change, I would not mind. After all, the paper itself did not have such a large readership anyway. So I shouldn't worry.

The next day, while sitting at my desk at work, I got an outside phone call from a lady purporting to be from downtown Cleveland and who said she had access to adoption records. She would neither tell me how she got my name nor how she got my phone number at work. All she wanted to know is would I be interested in her helping me get more information. I told her what little I knew about my birthmother and told her that I really didn't quite know if I'd want to meet her at this time. It seemed too odd to get such a precise phone call on the same day that the article appeared. She gave me her name and said she'd call me again sometime.

My wife then called me at work to tell me that the guy from the newspaper wanted to talk to me. Not only that, but my wife had already read the article; but instead of changing my name to something other than Larry, the reporter called me *Barry*. Not much camouflage there. In any case, my wife said, call him. It's about some lady who is looking for her birthparents and who wants to know if I can help her. Who's the lady who wants to know? Call the reporter.

I called the reporter. He said he had just hung up from talking to a lady who is looking for her birthparents and wanted to know if I could tell her how I had done my search. She might call again. No, he did not know her name. I called my wife. She said that the reporter called her about an hour before. "Mrs. Weeks," he said, "I have someone on the phone that read the article about your husband's search and wants to talk to him. Where does he work, Mrs. Weeks?" My wife told him and the reporter repeated the company's name as he wrote it down. When he picked up the other phone to tell the lady who called, there was no one there.

Now I was curious. What is going on? I called the Cleveland City Hall where adoption records are kept, and asked for the lady who called me. No such person with the name I was given exists. No, no one with a name anywhere close to that name worked there.

So, who was the lady? I figured that the lady read the article, called the newspaper reporter, and while he put the phone down to call my wife, was able to hear him say, "Mrs. Weeks, how can I contact Larry?" And when he repeated aloud the phone number that my wife gave to him, the mystery lady marked it down, hung up, and then called me. But still, who was the lady? Was she a friend of my adoptive mother who read the article? Or was it my birthmother or a friend of hers? My birthmother lived on the far west side of Cleveland and would have little chance of seeing this small newspaper. I knew that there was little or no chance of my adoptive mother reading it.

So, who was the lady? And what did she want? Was Elaine watching me? Had Elaine hired a detective or contacted a friend to call me and pump me for information?

The best I could ever figure about this mystery woman was that in late 1994 there was a *60 Minutes* or some such news report about a couple of ladies who had somehow obtained access to confidential adoption records in this part of the country and had gotten into legal trouble. It was mentioned that at one time the ringleader of these sneaky people had been in Cleveland offering her services, claiming to have access to confidential files. Perhaps one of them had read the article about my search and wanted to find out if I needed her help. Perhaps, but I never found out.

## Meanwhile

My search ground to a halt. I was still confident that I could at any time call the listings of the *James E. Lewises* (there were a couple of them on the west side) that were in the Cleveland phone book. I would go to sleep most nights mentally writing a letter to Elaine, convincing her that I was really her son, that she was really my mother, and that it would be nice for us to meet.

After all, by this time, I had adopted my second wife's daughter, Leslie; and my wife and I had our own son, Matthew. Therefore, my mother who was somewhere on the west side of Cleveland had a son, daughter-in-law, and three grandchildren whom she had never met.

Whenever there was a television talk show with the theme of reuniting adoptees with their parents, I would make sure to tape it. Then I would sit misty eyed, wondering what was going through their minds. I had read recent conflicting reports about the success of adoptee reunions. The adoptees had a right, I felt, to know about their parents; but the birthparents had a right to be left alone. This conflict kept me from going any further.

I knew I was a nice guy. But Elaine didn't know that. In fact, I didn't know if Elaine was anyone whom I would want to meet. Maybe she would be nasty, uncaring, divisive, and manipulative. Maybe she would be warm and loving, eager to re-establish contact. Delores, her former coworker and friend who used to work with Elaine had said nice things about her. That was reassuring.

Maybe the circumstances surrounding my birth were too sad or traumatic, and she wouldn't want to be reminded. Maybe she never told anyone about me; therefore, her secret had been safe. Did I have any right to interfere and reopen this drama?

What about my birthfather? Although I was less interested in him, for some reason, it nevertheless made me wonder if I could figure out who he was. I had little to go on.

> *"He had been in Service and was described as being in his early 30's and was of German heritage. It was stated that he had musical talent. He resided in his parental home . . . the biological father had been married previously."*

What would make a 20-year-old woman leave St. Paul, come to Cleveland, and live with people to whom she is probably not related? What if, I surmised, she came to Cleveland with my father because she was pregnant and her family back home had disowned her?

What if the family of my father offered to take care of her? If that were the case, perhaps one of the four families she roomed with in the 1943-44 city directory was my father's family.

But if she were to appear in the 1943-44 city directory, she would have had to be here late in 1942 or early 1943; because, I reasoned, I was conceived in

September 1943. My birth certificate said I was full-term.

Therefore, she came here before she got pregnant. But why? For jobs? There must have been many jobs back in St. Paul and Minneapolis. Maybe my father wanted her to come to Cleveland and room with his family until they got married. So, maybe one of the families in the four-unit apartment listed on my birth certificate had invited my birthfather and birthmother to stay with them.

And then, as the agency's information said, *"They (had) considered marriage but could not do so because of the fact that the biological father had been married previously."* Perhaps their intentions of getting married were dashed by Elaine's strong religious convictions. Rather than marry outside the church, she would give up my birthfather and give me up, too. A rather odd scenario, perhaps; but what else could one make of it?

- She went to the Catholic Church, told them that she was pregnant and wanted to marry the father of her baby.
- The Church said no—not in their church. He'd been married before. They could not sanction such a marriage.
- She chose to give me up rather than face the wrath of the Church.
- My birthfather moved on.

But then, *why didn't she tell the Church to hit the road, marry him in a civil wedding, and keep their child? Why didn't my father insist on that, too? How in the world could you give up a living, breathing child?*

A few more trips to the Cleveland Public Library showed that one of the families in that building back on Chatham Avenue had a son who was a veteran and who, in addition, used his parents' address as his own around the time I was born. Perhaps it was this young man who was my birthfather. But whom could I call? It was now in the late 1980s, and I'd be asking people to remember something from 40 years before. And what if I accidentally contacted the actual family of my birthfather and reopened wounds from years ago.

## The Search Continues

Armed with the local obituary for James E. Lewis, Elaine's only husband, I got out my Cleveland area map and found the tiny cemetery where he was buried. When I reached the cemetery, I noticed that it was a rather new-looking. There were no tall, old-looking tombstones. All the headstones were level with the ground. Here and there were occasional bouquets of flowers sticking out of the ground. Here and there were a few brown rectangles of dirt indicating a recent burial. I started looking around. Wouldn't that be something if Elaine were here right now, or what if she were to come here while I was looking for her husband's grave? But it was mid-afternoon, and no one but I was there.

I walked around and around and found nothing. There appeared to be no graves that were older than the late 1970s—years after James's death. So where was he buried? I went back to my map and double-checked its location. I was in the right place, wasn't I? But what's this? There, in the crease of the map was what looked like another cemetery with the same name. But it was farther down this little road.

About a half mile down the road, under a large tree-covered canopy, was an old-time cemetery . . . the kind that looks like a Hollywood cemetery: tombstones above the ground; tipped, broken, and worn-out tombstones; helter-skelter leaves; wrought-iron fences. And as I drove through the old cemetery, I could see that many stones were worn almost smooth over the years, and whoever was buried there was long forgotten. Not even a person's tombstone was eternal. And when was the last time anyone came by and paused to put a flower down or paused to say a prayer at the foot of these weather-beaten graves?

I parked in a cool, shady spot and started looking. The other cemetery was easier to go through. All those graves were in rather neat rows. The gravestones at this cemetery were here and there. Some were way over by the thick bushes ringing the east side of the cemetery. Others were lined up at the edge of a deep river ravine. I walked and walked. No grave was found for James Lewis.

I had gone up and down each section and felt ready to quit looking. I headed back toward my car. As I neared my car, about 30 feet away, right at the edge of the little gravel road, my eye was inexplicably drawn to a tombstone partially covered by a thick bush. There it was. The tombstone had James Lewis's name and also had Elaine's name. According to the stone's carvings, Elaine was still alive.

Here it was. I was standing at another place where my birthmother surely had been. And who knows how often she came here to reflect on James's death? I was moved. Another plateau had been reached in my search for Elaine, and I felt happy and satisfied that I was doing so well.

I said a few prayers for whoever James was. It was possible, I thought, that had she not given me up for adoption, this man would have been my stepfather. But my late adoptive father was a swell guy. What kind of man was James? Would he have liked me? Would I have liked him? The lady I knew who had been Elaine's friend years ago said very nice things about him. "They were overly generous, generous to a fault. Jim and Elaine would never hesitate to bring gifts over at Christmas. They were always eager to share."

I stood there quietly. I looked around for a landmark that would take me back to this spot again sometime. I wondered if I came here on an anniversary of James's death would I bump into Elaine. Or might she come the next day and miss me altogether? And then what would I say to her? Would I pretend to be visiting a grave nearby and strike up a casual conversation with her? Would she and I look enough alike that she would look at me and panic? And on and on my mind raced. The cemetery was over 40 miles from my home and would be difficult to visit on a regular basis. And wouldn't that be something if I came here and then left five minutes before Elaine came here? She apparently didn't have any relatives alive around Cleveland. Was she a frequent visitor?

I went to my car, got my camera, and took a picture of this rather direct link to Elaine. The cemetery was a quiet, peaceful place. The river could be heard skipping over and around the rocks at the bottom of the ravine. This place must be something in the fall with the changing leaves. I sighed. Then I left with a sense of accomplishment and a feeling of nervousness. I had come pretty close to Elaine, sort of in an indirect way, but close nonetheless. I just had to go further.

I now felt confident that I had Elaine's current address, former address, and knew where her husband was buried. Now I could back off a bit. I hoped if anything happened to Elaine that her friend would call me. Maybe not. I didn't know how close they were ever since Delores accidentally called her years ago.

I had to call her friend. Many years had gone by since I last spoke to her. Yes, Delores remembered me and always wondered what had happened with my search. Well, she hadn't spoken to Elaine since that day 15 years or so ago, but Elaine still sent her a Christmas card each year. I wondered about that. Why, if she was mad or embarrassed about that phone call years ago, would she keep in touch with this lady? Maybe deep down she didn't want to lose contact with this lady who had spoken to her son. She said she didn't want to really give me any direct information. I understood. I told her that I had continued my search and had come to an impasse. I knew a few things about Elaine that I didn't know before. Like what, she asked? Well, Elaine Lewis's husband James is buried in a small cemetery in Olmsted Falls. I had been there.

"What did you say?" she gasped. I no sooner got the name Elaine *Lewis* out and her friend gasped. "How did you know her last name was *Lewis*? I never gave you that information," she insisted. "How did you find out Elaine's married name?"

"You told me," I answered. "A long time ago you told me that she married the brother-in-law of the owner of a house she roomed in. And, armed with that little, teeny-weeny clue, it took me less than a half a morning at the Cleveland Public Library to find out to whom she was married and when her only husband had died."

Her friend was shocked. "Oh my God! How could you have done all that with just that little bit of information?"

"Just curious I guess," I answered. I also told her that I knew that she currently lived in a city near the Cleveland airport. When I told her the address I had, she was silent, neither confirming nor denying. I had hoped she'd say that I was right. But now she knew that just a little crumb of information might become a whole loaf to this very inquisitive guy.

Again, I asked her questions about Elaine. What did she look like? She was short, with light-colored hair. Was she intelligent, well dressed, well read? Did she smoke? Did she drink? Was she a conservative thinker or liberal? Wondering how much I could get that would sculpt a picture of Elaine, I buzzed her with anything I could think of.

She told me that Elaine was intelligent, well dressed; but she didn't quite remember if Elaine smoked or not. Probably not. She socially drank. She was a hard worker. She was judgmental and opinionated. If you crossed her, she'd never let you forget it. If she liked you, there was nothing she wouldn't do.

Elaine once had a parrot. She liked cats. She liked crossword puzzles. Elaine introduced her to coffee and ever since then, Delores was a coffee drinker. And on and on.

Try as I might, I had a hard time visualizing her. Do you have any pictures of her? After a little thought, she said that, yes, somewhere down in the basement were pictures of her from years ago. Next time she goes down to the basement, she'll bring them up. Call her in a few weeks.

How's about if she called Elaine, her friend suggested, invited her to go somewhere for lunch, and then I could show up and get to see her? Not a bad idea, I thought. Could be risky. How's about if you just plain call her? After all, years have gone by. The last time you spoke to her was about this bizarre charge of having given up a baby years ago. If she called her now, Elaine would have to want to bring up that long-ago phone call, wouldn't she?

If Elaine did *not* bring it up, then something would be wrong. Maybe Elaine's silence all these years indicated that she was hoping that this guy who called her friend was totally wrong. Maybe he had the wrong mother. If so, then her secret would continue to be safe. Maybe she felt that the less attention made to the phone call, the more people would forget it.

Unfortunately, I spent a few months waiting for her friend to go to her basement to retrieve the photos and months waiting for her friend to call Elaine. It was obvious to me that she really did not want to get involved in any of this. So, I decided to use her friend just for casual information about Elaine. After all, this nice lady was interested in this story, but Delores really didn't want to be the one who made the big contact. Fair enough.

## The Search Speeds Up

Almost every night, I would go to sleep silently composing the ultimate letter to Elaine. *"Dear Elaine Margaret Vincent, I am Joseph Allan Vincent who was born..."* And I would eventually fall asleep. My wife didn't know what I was thinking while I lay there waiting to doze off. It was my private little letter. And each time I started the mental letter, it got longer and more precise. I was, I felt, just a letter, just a phone call away from contacting this person. That close. And it was all up to me as to when I'd go forward.

Most people with whom I talked thought it was neat. Wow! Looking for someone after all these years. Have you met her? No. Don't you want to? I don't know. Maybe she's someone I wouldn't want to meet. Don't you just want to knock on the door and pretend that you're selling something? Yes. Wouldn't you like to just stand across the street and look at her? Yes, yes, yes. But the time's not right. I was a cautious guy, too cautious to stumble into a possibly bad situation. Besides (and this was a "big" *besides)*, my adoptive mother was still alive. I didn't want her to find out. She'd be very unhappy to find out about such a search. No, no, the time was not right.

One day my oldest daughter, Yvette, whose birth had launched this search back in 1968, became intensely interested in these goings-on and asked me if I knew where Elaine Lewis lived. I gave her the address that I had figured out years before. It's not too far from where Elaine and her late husband lived, I told her. She must have sold the house and moved. Had I ever seen the new house? No. Why didn't I drive over and see what it looks like?

I took a vacation day and drove my Astro van to the lower west side Cleveland suburb of Middleburg Heights and, being pretty good with maps, was driving down her street within an hour. The street even had an Indian name: *Cherokee Trail*. I parked two houses away from the address and stared at the two-story home on a quiet street. Neat lawns, clean sidewalks. Very nice. I took out my camera and got ready to take a picture. But this was mid-day—the sun was shining. What would neighbors say if they spotted a strange van parked on their street with some guy with a camera sitting in it? They'd probably call the cops. I decided to go for a walk.

I got out of the car, pretended that I belonged on the street, and began walking down the street toward that particular house. I slowed my gait a bit and nonchalantly gazed at my target house. I had better gaze at the rest of the houses on the street in the same way, or someone will wonder what's going on. I studied the house. All the doors were closed. No lights were on. No car in the driveway. Probably at work (she'd be in her early 70s now) or volunteering somewhere. Or maybe she's sleeping. I walked all the way around the block, noting which house was hers when I got on the street behind. I could see just a little of her back yard . . . not much though.

I imagined that I could see her puttering around back there, tending flowers, and watering her garden. I imagined I could see her. She'd look up at the guy on the street behind her who was staring at her. She'd look down and away and resume her separate life, not thinking anything of the fellow on the block behind her.

I walked slowly around the block, got back into my van, and set the camera on the dashboard. I pulled into the driveway of her house, aimed the camera, and clicked the shutter. Wouldn't that have been something if she was staring out just then? Wow!

When I got home, I called my daughter and told her that I had seen the house. I even took a picture. Nice house. No signs of life, though. What's next? I don't know.

A couple days later, Yvette called me and told me that she called the number in the phone book. She used some sort of innocent pretense, but it appeared that I had the *wrong* address. Whoever answered the phone, she explained, sounded very young. Since I knew she didn't have any family around here, I had no explanation as to why the person sounded young. Somehow Yvette couldn't get the lady to admit that she had lived there quite a while.

In other words, *I had the wrong house*. I had taken a picture of the wrong house. Whoever lived there had a husband with the same name as Elaine's late husband, but that was it. No, this was a young couple; and, obviously, I wasn't the slightest bit closer to finding Elaine.

Back to the library. I took out the most current phone book and wrote down every name listed for *James E. Lewis, James Lewis, Jas. Lewis, J. Lewis,*

*Elaine Lewis,* and *E. Lewis.* For hours and hours I stared at the list. Was she listed or unlisted in the phone book? I checked the location of each phone number and eliminated those people who did not live on Cleveland's west side. My list got smaller and smaller. There was, however, an *E. Lewis* who lived near the airport; and I bet that that was my Elaine. No doubt about it. I was tempered, of course, by the fact that for about ten years, I had the wrong address. What if I had mailed those people that *ultimate* letter?

## Documentation Search Begins

Now I was approaching my 50th birthday. A half-century had gone by, and Elaine and I were still separate beings and apparently destined to continue to be separate. Since I remembered that Elaine's friend told me that my birthmother was born in early May, I took a long shot and wrote to the Minnesota Bureau of Vital Statistics to see if I could get a birth certificate for Elaine. After all, I could give them a name, a month, and a year. I gave it a try.

A couple weeks later I got her birth certificate. For the first time in my life I knew that her middle name was Marie (not *Margaret* as I had suspected), her dad's name was Fred, her mom's name was Alvina, she was the *fourth* child of that marriage; and it even listed their address on the day she was born. If I were to start drawing a biological family tree, I could now list my birthmother's full name and both of my birth-grandparents.

I wanted more. It also told me that they were from a city called *Little Canada* that was in Minnesota. I checked my atlas and found Little Canada to be a speck, a tiny circle above St. Paul. It looked like a suburb—a teeny-weeny one. I called information and got the address of the city hall in Little Canada. Maybe they had some information about my birth-grandparents. Maybe not. But I fired off a letter, put it in the mailbox, and eagerly awaited a reply.

A week later, I got a letter from a woman in Little Canada who said she turned my letter over to a

*Vincent* specialist who would get back to me as soon as she could. There was, she said, a great deal of *Vincent* information available.

Meanwhile, I wrote to the St. Paul Public Library and asked them if they could photostat copies of the 1910, 1920, 1940, and 1950 city directory for *Vincents*. I reasoned that in 1910 there might be a listing of my birth-grandparents, 1920 definitely should list them (after all, my birthmother was born in 1922, was the fourth child), 1940 might list Elaine's older brothers, sisters, and parents, and 1950 would let me know, by their absence, if her parents had moved or perhaps died.

And sure enough, a week or two later, I got an envelope with four pages of photostats. The 1920 city directory page showed that, yes, my birth-grandparents lived at the same address that was on Elaine's birth certificate. And, additionally, it showed that my birth grandfather was a milk wagon driver for the Minnesota Milk Company.

They didn't have a 1940 city directory listing, but they sent 1941's. Interestingly, it showed that Elaine's mother Alvina was listed as the widow of Fred. In the 1950 directory, Alvina disappears altogether. Basically, what I could guess was that her husband (my grandfather) had died somewhere between 1922 (Elaine's birthday) and 1941. It was an 18-year window of time, but at least I could narrow it down.

Next stop? The Western Reserve Historical Society near downtown Cleveland. Sorry, sir, but the most current census information available is 1920.

Yes, we have the St. Paul census on microfilm. The government requires a 72-year waiting period before they'll allow you to see census data. But the 1920 census would certainly be helpful.

And it was. After a two-hour search, I found Fred and Alvina's census data that told me how old they were, their occupations (milk wagon driver and housewife, so that checked out), their children's names (those born before 1920: Joyce M. and Fred J., Jr.), and even where Fred's and Alvina's parents came from. Since Elaine was the fourth child, I needed to know who the third one was. Each of these little doors was opening to more little doors. And every time a door opened, my birth-family tree got bigger and bigger.

## My 50th Birthday

I decided that on my 50th birthday, I would take the day off work, drive to the west side, visit that lone address where I had guessed that Elaine lived, walk down the street and say to myself, "I have finally found her home 50 years to the day that I was born." It would be a fitting occasion and would be difficult to forget—something to write about someday. Plus, I'll visit her husband's grave while I'm in the neighborhood.

I took the day off, drove to the west side of Cleveland, and found the little Berea neighborhood with the *E. Lewis* address. These homes were smaller, older, and quainter. I parked at the end of the street after making sure I found her address, got out, and started a leisurely stroll. Yes, here on a sunny summer workday, a 50-year-old man was walking down his birthmother's street. This address had to be the right one. Definitely.

As I approached the yard, I got nervous. I'm sure the pupils of my eyes were at their largest. I slowed a little as I neared the driveway. There in the back yard and on the driveway in front of the garage were lots of children's toys. I knew Elaine didn't have any grandchildren other than mine. So whose toys were they? Was I wrong again? I guess I was wrong again.

Since I was in the vicinity, I drove to the house that Elaine and James had shared when he died, the home mentioned in James' obituary. Although years ago I thought that the address was wrong since I couldn't find it in the directory, I had discovered that their address was listed in a different city's directory. Their street was actually in two cities. I found their former home on a corner lot and took a picture. It looked like a nice home with a big yard. Lots of grass to cut. Probably too big to take care of. That's probably why she moved.

I drove home with mixed feelings. I probably had the wrong address again. A simple phone call that went to an answering machine proved that the *E* in *E. Lewis* was actually *Elizabeth*. So once again, I was wrong. But I tried. That's what counted. So what I thought would be a real neat 50th birthday event turned out to be a wrong turn. Undeterred, I moved on in my search.

My wife put on a 50th birthday party for me and invited quite a few people. My best friend Ray, whom I had known since I was a kid and with whom I shared my search experiences, gave me a computer program called *Family Tree Maker*©. After everyone went home that night, I loaded the program; and then I began putting in the meager data that I had collected. I then put my wife's family tree into the computer. I had done her family tree years ago and had done all the work by hand. Extensive as it was (I had her traced back to the 1500s), I never thought I would ever find out that much about my birth family.

However, a week later I got a thick 10" x 14" envelope in the mail. Inside was a letter from a lady in Little Canada who had access to a lot of *Vincent* information. "We might be relatives," she suggested. She had enclosed an incredible amount of family-group sheets for all kind of *Vincents*. I was astonished.

Eagerly, I began loading the sheets into my new computer software; and slowly it became obvious that I was indeed related to the people in this pack of paper. My birth-grandfather was listed on a sheet with information about his siblings and both parents. Handwritten in a circle next to Frederick's name was *"10 children."* Wow! He was the oldest of ten children, and then he himself had ten children. Now I knew when he and his brothers and sisters were born. I knew I had a challenge to find who his ten children were. I knew of three at this point: Joyce M., the oldest; Frederick J., the second child; and Elaine, the fourth child. The rest would prove to be a mystery that would slowly unfold over the next few months.

After all the data were in the computer, I found out that my source of information back in Little Canada, Minnesota, was in fact, according to the program, my "third cousin twice removed." Not knowing what that really meant, I was at least impressed that my source of information from far, far away was a blood relative. I wrote to her, told her the story of my search, and stressed that I, at this point, had not met Elaine. Nor did anyone in Elaine's family know anything about my search. My newly found relative promised secrecy and encouraged me to continue. Through the next few months, she forwarded all sorts of family sheets, calendars, and obituaries that helped me to construct a list of at least eight of the ten children of my grandparents.

The obituaries were particularly helpful because they generally listed brothers and sisters in chronological order. So, you could get names and the order of birth from simple little obituaries. I had to guess when the various brothers and sisters of my birthmother were born.

The obituaries also gave me a new mystery. I knew from Elaine's friend that she married only once. Therefore she was *Elaine Vincent* until she married and became *Elaine Lewis*. But in the obituary for her little sister Rita Marie, who died at the age of 12 in 1946 in St. Paul, Elaine was listed as Mrs. Elaine *Baker*. Who was *Baker*? Had she been married? I reasoned that perhaps, since she was listed in 1944 on my birth certificate as *Elaine Vincent*, she got married to somebody named *Baker*, and then he either died or divorced her. Elaine must have come back to St. Paul for her sister's funeral either married to or pretending to be married to someone named *Baker*. Since she was listed in 1951 as *Vincent*, she must have been married for a very short time. But why then wasn't she *Elaine Baker* in the subsequent city directory listings? It seemed like every time I cleared up a mystery, another would unfold.

## Getting Warm

In a few short months, I had constructed a family tree database of almost 900 names, numerous dates and places—an incredible amount of information about a family of which I was a biological part. But I didn't know if I'd ever meet any of them. I had hundreds of ancestors' names, the names of most of Elaine's brothers and sisters, her father's death certificate, Elaine's birth certificate, her brothers' baptism information, obituaries on a couple of her siblings; and yet, even though these were real people, they were all so far away. I felt like I was looking through a window into a house in which you really belonged, but a place into which you dared not go.

A story emerged of a young, struggling family with lots of children: My grandfather died in 1940, barely 45 years old, of liver failure, more than likely due to excessive drinking, leaving a widow with ten children and obviously lots of hardship.

After Elaine's father died in 1940, her brother Gerald died in the service in 1944. Then in 1944, I was born and she gave me up for adoption, and in 1946 her young sister Rita died of a bowel obstruction. Obviously, the 1940s were not good for her. There must have been a great deal of pathos and sorrow.

I surmised that she then came to Cleveland in 1943, got pregnant, couldn't marry my father, felt she couldn't go home due to the financial conditions back in St. Paul, gave me up for adoption, married someone named *Baker*, divorced, changed her name back to

*Vincent*, married again in 1963, had a serious cancer operation, got widowed in 1972, and now lives alone in Cleveland barely 40 miles away from me. And still we go our separate ways.

And maybe we've passed on a crowded street in Cleveland. Or maybe we've stood at the same counter in some big store waiting for a clerk. Or perhaps we passed at a ball game. Maybe we were stopped at a red light sitting in cars side by side. Maybe we laughed at the same Sunday comics. Or maybe we were in church and prayed for each other at the same time. Maybe. Maybe not.

Now what? What do I do with all this? I was too afraid to make an attempt at a meeting. Besides, I didn't really know exactly where she lived. Only one person knew that: her friend Delores. I needed to know. I called her friend.

"Well, how's it going in your search?" Elaine's friend asked.

"I've run of out of gas," I answered. "I had narrowed it down to a few areas of Greater Cleveland where she might be living; but if she's not listed in the phone book, I can't go any further," I admitted.

"Well, you know," she said, "she moved after her husband Jimmy died. And she didn't really move too far."

"Do you remember," I reminded her, "that you said you were thinking of calling Elaine?"

"Yeah, I have her address here somewhere. Her phone number is in my book. I really should call her. I've been meaning to call her for a long time. And not just about this. You know, I just have to go out and have coffee with her sometime."

I agreed that that was a good idea. "Please do it," I thought impatiently to myself.

"You know," her friend told me, "she lives on a street that I can't even find on my AAA map."

"A new address?" I asked.

"No, the same one she moved to years ago. I was thinking of calling up and going to visit her, but I can't find the street."

"What's the name of the street?" I asked, hoping that she'd let it slip.

"Oh no, Larry," she laughed. "You want me to tell you the street name. I can't do that. I'm sure that you'll be able to find out on your own. I'm not being mean, but I just don't want her to think that I invaded her privacy."

I told her that I understood completely. Sorry about my feeble attempt to get her to slip. Rats! I almost had it.

Since I knew that Elaine was not listed anywhere, and her friend confirmed that, then the phone book or any other kind of directory would be useless. But what kind of street would not appear on a map? New streets maybe. But she didn't live on a new street. Her friend said she had lived there for a while. Maybe a street so small, like in a condominium development or a trailer park.

## The Powwow and Narrowing Gap

My daughter Yvette, who was studying anthropology at Cleveland State University, called me one day and told me that the strangest thing happened. She went to a powwow. What was that? Well, a bunch of students, faculty, and anyone else who's interested gets together for American Indian dances, ceremonies, craft displays, and any other related things—kind of an anthropological Indian culture orgy. After I told Yvette that she was part Indian, she became interested in anything dealing with Native Americans. And, as yet, we still didn't know how much Indian blood was flowing in our veins.

And there she sat in the stands, she said, watching the ceremonies; and three little old ladies came in and sat right next to her. "And one of the ladies, the one in the middle, looked exactly like you, Dad. Exactly!" Yvette said. "So I sat there staring at her. And she stared back at me. Really, Dad. Looked just like you."

So, later, during one of the intermissions, one of the other sweet little ladies spoke to the look-alike lady and called her *Elaine*! "I was in shock, Dad. *Elaine*!"

"Well then what happened?"

"I just sat there staring at her, Dad!"

"Why didn't you politely nudge the lady next to you and ask her what the lady in the middle's last name was? Even if it were *Lewis*, you could say, 'Oh, I'm sorry. She just kind of looked like someone I knew.' Or, why didn't you follow them out to the parking lot after the powwow to see if the lady in question got behind the wheel. Then you'd know it was her car. And you'd have a license plate number you could check." Oh well, if I'd been there, I probably would have frozen up, too. All kinds of things can be thought of when it's too late to do them.

But what about this street that didn't appear on a regular map? And it was not too far from where Elaine lived with her late husband, said her friend. I went to the library and photocopied from a book, the street map for the city where she supposedly lived. Lots of streets. If the street appears on this map, why wouldn't it appear on a bigger map? And I stared and stared. New street? No, her friend said she lived there for a while. Apartment or condo complex? I didn't know of any on the east side of Cleveland that had unlisted street names. So why wouldn't they have one for the west side.

But this lady said that she was using a AAA map. Maybe the map was one of those that you unfold into a huge sheet. Those maps wouldn't necessarily list each and every street. I noticed that the map I was looking at showed a trailer park, a rather large one. A trailer park? No, her friend would have said the words *trailer* or *trailer park* sometime in her discussions with me. Unless she didn't even know that Elaine lived in a trailer. That was possible. Besides, all she'd gotten from Elaine all these years was a Christmas card. And she said that she never really did go to visit her since Elaine's husband had died. That was long ago.

Let's try again. I called her friend Delores. "No, I had not found out anything new. I'm kinda' stuck. Have you tried to call her for a reunion?"

"No, never quite got around to it. And, ya' know, I never got around to going through the stuff in the basement to find your mother's picture," she confessed.

I knew I wasn't getting too far with her friend. Either Delores didn't want to help me and didn't know how to tell me, or her life was so busy that my situation was not of any priority. She seemed nice though, and she always sounded as if she would just love to go one word further to tell me where Elaine lived. But she just couldn't do it.

So, all I could do was ask her things about Elaine. I sat there at the phone with a pad of paper and wrote everything down as she spoke. To verify what she'd told me months before, I'd repeat an occasional question.

Was Elaine maintaining this subtle contact once a year to show that the accusation from years ago was false? If so, she could act like nothing happened. Or maybe Elaine was maintaining this annual connection in case that young man who was looking for her wanted to use her friend as an intermediary. What was going through Elaine's mind each year when she sent a Christmas card to a friend who one day—years ago—called her to tell her that there's some guy who says he's your son? If she were a proud woman, she'd probably not want to keep in touch.

I would imagine that, if Delores actually called her on the phone, in a matter of minutes, very few minutes, she'd find out what Elaine thought about that call years before. I doubted that Elaine would pretend that the call was forgotten. But here was Elaine's friend, out of touch for 15 years or so, who kept in Christmas card contact with her. One call, one simple call, would reveal so much. But I couldn't get the lady to make the call, to find pictures of Elaine, or to go to visit Elaine. So my only contact was feeble at best.

During one of our phone calls, her friend sounded like she wanted to let the cats out of the bag—all of them. She sounded as if she were weakening. She sounded as if she just had to, just once, give me just one more clue, something. And she did. While discussing the fact that she wouldn't be able to visit Elaine if she'd want to because the street wasn't on the map, her friend let slip the name of Elaine's street, *Elgin Oval*. Once she had let the name slip, she sounded relieved. "Well, it won't do you much good, Larry, because she's not listed in the phone book anyway. You probably won't be able to find it anyway." Hah! Don't bet on it!

Zoom. Off I went to the library. *Elgin Oval*. "A big break in the case," as the detective would say. Give me a crumb, and I'll have a loaf. My confidence soared. And there it was, *Elgin Oval*, sitting smack dab in the middle of a trailer park—a huge trailer park. But her friend was right: how would I find out where she lived if her address was unlisted? Details! Details!

I looked for the *Elgin Oval* Street in the *Haines Directory*, which lists, in address order, the people on each street. All the streets are listed alphabetically. So, all I had to do was look for *Elgin Oval* and then see what that would lead to. There it was. A street with 28 trailers. Six of the trailers listed had no names or phone numbers—just x's. These x's were the unlisted people. Elaine lived in one of those six 'x' listings. I had narrowed Elaine's home on the entire planet earth down to a street and six homes on that street. Not bad, huh?

## Bingo!

I had Elaine's street. I used to know just her city. Now I had her street. Were her ears ringing? Was she getting premonitions that something was going on? Did she have any idea that there was this kind of activity going on regarding herself?

I figured that I should drive over to the trailer park and just toddle down the little street where she lived. I knew exactly which six addresses were unlisted. Maybe the trailer park made the people put their names on each mailbox. That would be helpful. What if they didn't have names on the mailboxes? I didn't care. I just wanted to say that I had actually driven on her street past one of the six unlisted addresses, one of which was hers. And what if I saw her? Who knew? Let's just get going!

Off I went. It was about forty miles to the trailer park. I drove right past the trailer park on my first try because it sets away from the main road and is not all that obvious. But I turned around and pulled into the little entrance road. Now I sensed trouble. There in front of me was a guard shack with, what else, a guard! I pulled over to the side to think.

Hmmm. If I pull up and say I'm here to see Elaine Lewis, the lady might want to know who I am. Or she might let me go in, and then she might call Elaine to say that she's having company. Or worse . . . *it might be Elaine in the guard shack.* I didn't know what she looked like. I'd be asking *Elaine* to see

*Elaine*. She might have gotten a job in that very guard shack. That might be Elaine sitting right there.

Something caused me to put my car in gear, and my car rolled toward the shack. A sweet-looking little old lady peeked through a screened window.

"May I help you?" asked the little old lady.

"I'm here to drop off a gift," said I. A couple cars pulled up behind me. I looked at the lady in the booth.

"At what address, sir?" She had not given up.

I have no idea what I was thinking; but I suddenly blurted out that if I saw my friend's car, I'd know where he lived. Does that make any sense? Of course not. But, with a few cars lined up behind me, and not being eager to pursue this pointless interrogation, she said, "OK, go through." No argument here. I put it in gear and pressed forward.

Now I was in the park driving through a maze of narrow, winding little roads. Trailers were everywhere. I had never seen so many trailers. But this whole complex looked like a huge village. There were lots of trees, walkways, a set of trolley tracks, more trees, more trailers, and park benches. The trees were old. They'd been there for years. Around and around I drove. I'll never find my way out. More turns. More little streets; and, over to the left, almost missed by my discerning eye, was *Elgin Oval*. I pulled out my list of *Elgin Oval* addresses. I had the unlisted address numbers memorized. Let's go. I made a slow left turn onto *Elgin Oval*, a cute little street that had a slight curve. Each trailer had a little yard. A few trees were here and there. Each trailer had a little driveway leading to a carport. I looked at my list again. The first one without a listing was the *37* address. And I also noticed that the 37 mailbox had a name made of metal that sat atop the peak. I nudged forward and—

*There it was!* My search was over! The second mailbox from the corner had, in white metal letters, *E. LEWIS* sitting right on top. This was her trailer! My 26-year search was over. I had found her home. I was right in front of it. I was looking at her trailer. This was her place of residence. And if I sat here any longer, she'd wonder whose car that was out there and call that sweet lady in the guard shack to tell her that some car is lurking around outside her trailer. I moved down the street very slowly. I didn't see any sign of life in the trailer. I couldn't see any lights on at all. There was no car in the little driveway. Maybe she was at work. Maybe she was inside sleeping or watching TV. Maybe she was at the store. Maybe . . .

I couldn't just sit there. My long search was essentially over. Of all the places on this planet for Elaine to live, I had found the exact spot. I turned around, went back toward her trailer, pulled up to the corner stop sign, and paused. Visible in my rear-view mirror (because of the little curve in the road) was the image of her trailer. I just stared. Here I was, closer to the woman who gave birth to me than I had ever been—just a few feet away. And I was looking at her home.

I pulled forward, made a right turn, drove down a million little winding lanes, and somehow found my way out of the trailer park. At the main road, I turned right and went down toward where Elaine used to live. I wanted to visit her late husband's grave while I was there. I needed to reflect on how far I'd come. What better place to do so.

Not too far down the road and a couple of left turns, later I came to the cemetery and pulled up to James Lewis's grave. Now I could rest a bit in my search. I had found his widow. Right now I was within a mile or so of her home. And here I was standing at her husband's grave.

There next to the grave, over by a bush, someone had discarded a bouquet of artificial flowers. I picked up the plastic bouquet and took it over to James's grave. I pushed the metal point of the plastic bouquet into the soft ground in front of his headstone. Wouldn't she wonder, I thought, who put this plastic flower here? But then, maybe some kids would come along and take it anyway.

The long drive home was a pensive one. I put on some thinking-type music and thought about the long road I'd come down and how successful I had been with a lot of determination, some good clues, and an indescribable urge to continue. And how a desire to search for my roots 26 years ago, while I held my first-born daughter, had led me this far. I hadn't taken the big, big step yet—attempting to contact her. But I could rest assured that I knew exactly where to go when the time came. I was proud of myself. I was emotionally drained, but I was pleased and apprehensive.

I immediately called my daughter Yvette and told her of my success. She was thrilled. She said she wanted to drive out there, too. She'd see if she could see a person, a car, a license plate, or something. Maybe that would tell us more.

The next week Yvette called me from Olmsted Township, Elaine's city. She was lost. When she left the trailer park, Yvette forgot where to get back onto the freeway. Not only that, but she made a fool of herself at the notorious guard shack.

I was pretty sure I had told her that she would be asked whom she was visiting in the park. Well, Yvette pulled up to the guard shack. Yes, can we help you? I'm here to see my grandmother, said Yvette. What's her name? Yvette thought for a second. I don't know my grandmother's last name, but I'll know her car if I see it. Cars were stacking up behind Yvette's car. Well, the lady thought, OK, go on in. And surprisingly Yvette, with a little fast (but nutty) thinking, had escaped the guard shack, too. Yvette didn't see any sign of life at Elaine's trailer, but she did see a beige station wagon. It was parked back far enough that she couldn't see the license plate.

Boy, Yvette. Only *you* would tell someone that not only didn't you know your own granny's name, but that you would recognize her car. Maybe Granny was not one of your favorite people, the lady in the guard shack probably thought.

But somehow Yvette got in the park. She said she was tempted to go up to the door of the trailer and pass herself off as a salesman. I could just hear Yvette fumbling for words and saying, "Hi, I'm working my way through magazines selling colleges." Perhaps the park had restrictions on solicitors that would get her in trouble. I agreed that we both wanted to see what she looked like, but we'd better be more cautious. In any case, we were getting close . . . too close . . . to the ultimate goal. And now what to do?

## Writing The Letter

What to do next? With the impetuousness of youth, my daughter Yvette was becoming more and more involved in the search for Elaine. We both agreed that it was nice that we at least knew where she was. And since Yvette and I were still in frequent contact with my adoptive mother and sister, we knew we were playing with fire. We both agreed not to say anything to my adoptive family about what we had done. I assured Yvette that I had no intention of telling them. This would have to be our secret.

I thought about the whole thing for a few weeks. It was now autumn of 1994, a reflective time of the year. Leaves were falling. Cleveland Browns football. Lots of colors. Nature's banquet for the eyes. And I still went to sleep each night mentally writing the big letter to Elaine, the one that would convince her to want to know me.

For years, I had been working on the big letter. In my computer I had composed a long letter with all the details of my search. Once she'd read my letter, I reasoned, she'd just have to meet me. Every so often I'd go into my computer letter and rewrite this and reword that, take out this paragraph, and put in that one. The letter grew and grew.

The few people with whom I had shared my story were insistent that I go ahead and try to effect a meeting. "The time's not right," I'd say.

"You'll never know if you don't try," they'd answer.

"I don't have a right to invade her privacy," I'd reply.

"Go ahead," they'd say. And on and on and on. My brother-in-law said I was just looking for excuses. He was right.

What would happen if my adoptive mother and sister found out? That was probably my biggest worry. I didn't think it was their business anyway, and I didn't want to face a barrage of nasty questions and comments. I just knew that they, in no way, would tolerate such a breech of family loyalty. Had my adoptive mother passed away years ago, I'm sure I would have gone ahead and tried to make contact with Elaine a lot sooner. Basically, I didn't want to hurt anyone: my adoptive mother, my sister, my daughter Yvette, myself.

But one thing kept sticking in my mind: We weren't getting any younger. I was 50 years old; Elaine was 72. Almost twenty years or so ago, she knew I was looking for her. Back then she was in her mid-50s. I was then in my early 30s. All those years had passed; and yet, for many reasons, we were still separated. But we were not getting any younger. That was important. If I waited 15 more years, she'd be in her late 80s or dead, and I'd be in my mid 60s or dead. If I were to meet her on this side of death, I had best move on and give it a try.

I went back to my trusty computer. I looked at the size of the letter that I had written over the past years. Too big. Too imposing. Too scary. Too much information. If she were to get that bulky, data-jammed monster in her mailbox, it would probably scare the hell out of her. I opened a new file in the computer. I started from scratch. And the words flowed:

## The Letter

*Dear Elaine Lewis:*

*I'm not sure how to start this letter, so I'll just let my fingers begin. It is not my intention to hurt anyone, so I hope that you will understand that my motives are pure and that I find it as difficult to write this as it is difficult for you to read this.*

*I am Joseph Allan Vincent, born to Elaine Vincent at 5:10 p.m., on Thursday, June 15, 1944. Elaine was a single mother who lived at 3115 Chatham Avenue on Cleveland's near west side. She lived in a four-family unit but was not the main occupant of any of the units. The 1943-44 Cleveland city directory lists Patrick and Rita Snyder in Apt #1, Henry E. Hall in Apt #2, George and Lottie Condol in Apt #3, and Harold E. Chinn in Apt #4. Elaine apparently lived with one of those families and worked at HPL Mfg.*

*Elaine does not appear in the city directory in 1947. She does, however, appear in the 1951 directory, apparently rooming with Joseph and Carolyn Levy on West 61st St. Carolyn Levy was the sister of Fran Czaban who used to own a small Mom and Pop store with her husband Lester at 2906 Chatham Avenue, on the next corner just across the street from where Eliane lived while she carried me.*

*In 1955 Elaine moves in with the Lester Czaban family on Camden Avenue (Lester was now a driver for Leisy Brewery) and then in 1958 moves with them to West 90th St. In 1961 and 1963 Elaine is listed as having lived in Bay Village. After 1963 Elaine does* *not appear any more in the city directories. Perhaps in 1963 or 1964, Elaine marries. In 1972 Elaine is listed in obituaries as the widow of James E. Lewis who was the brother of both Carolyn Levy and Frances Levy (Pawlak). The <u>Plain Dealer</u> and <u>Berea Sun Times</u> obituaries show "James E. Lewis, beloved husband of Elaine (nee Vincent)."*

*After a great deal of legwork and research, I have found the person who I believe to be my biological mother. Please keep in mind, Elaine, that I am not some nosey little kid. I am a mature 50-year-old man, husband and father of 3 wonderful children (two girls- 26 and 19, and one 14-year-old red-haired boy). I have a bachelor's degree from Cleveland State majoring in American History. I am currently an instructor of English and personal computers at a private college in Lake County. I am heavily into genealogy, having helped trace my wife Renee's family back to the early 1500s.*

*I tried to get information from Catholic Charities, but they gave me next to nothing. If I wanted any details, I was told that I would have to get a court order to release the file. All they would tell me was that my mother was in her early twenties, French-Canadian, and part Indian. They also said that she met my father at an army camp and that she wanted to marry him, but because he had already been divorced, she would not be able to marry in the church. Therefore, they said, she elected to give me up for adoption.*

*I am a God-fearing, formerly auburn-haired, sensitive, loving, and cautious man. It is possible that you will become very upset at this letter. If so, I apologize, Elaine. I also hope that you will take some time to think about what I am asking for, and I hope that you will show understanding and compassion. I only want to meet you, at least once, and then let God decide if it will be any longer.*

*You will be 73 next year, and I will be 51. It could be possible to create a friendship through our reunion that might be rewarding. Again, Elaine, I am a mild-mannered and gentle man who wants little but to meet you. It may seem like a lot to you. You have been guaranteed anonymity by the State of Ohio; but, on the other hand, you gave birth to a tenacious and curious little guy.*

*Basically, this is what I'm proposing: Re-read this letter and think about meeting me. You could have an intermediary present—a priest or a close friend. You could write me a letter telling me about yourself and avoid meeting me altogether. I'll understand. Or you could write to me and agree to meeting me face to face. I want nothing more than to see you and to have you tell me for hours all about yourself.*

*I am Joseph Allan Vincent born June 15, 1944. There's no doubt about that. And unless I'm really missing something, you are Elaine Vincent, the 22-year old young lady who gave me up during wartime when I was a baby. Such a meeting and any resulting friendship could be just between the two of us; no one else need know—no one.*

*Elaine, I've written and re-written this letter for years now. I've gone to bed thousands of nights men-*

*tally composing these lines. Ever since you were accidentally contacted in 1976, I have felt awful that someone other than me contacted you. It was never my intention for you to be confronted like you were. Their intentions were good, but you should not have been approached out of the blue like you were. And ever since then, I've been scared about repeating any hurt you might have had. But it's 18 years later. I personally don't think that there is any one best time to send this to you. I'll never know if you'd be receptive to meeting me if I don't try to do so. I've let 18 years go by that cannot be replaced. And now being a 50-year old adult makes me all the more anxious to do so. I just wonder if you think about who I am and what I'm doing as much as I wonder the same things about you.*

*If you think this is too much or entirely out of the question, then I will abide by your decision. But if you are as curious as I am, then we will both gain from such contact. I hope you will pray a lot before you decide whether to answer me or not. Whatever you decide, I promise that I will continue to pray for you and hope that the good Lord will bless you for giving me a chance to have a wonderful family like I have. Please write to me some day and let me know what you would like to do. Bless you.*

*Cautiously optimistic and lovingly curious,*

*Lawrence Andrew Weeks*

## The Wait

But I didn't mail it immediately. I read it, read it again, put it in an envelope, and addressed it to the new, for-sure address I had. Put a stamp on it. After teaching night school one evening, I drove to the post office; pulled up to the drive-up mailbox, and . . . I stopped. Since it was 10:30 p.m., there were no other cars in the parking lot. I rolled down my window, stuck out my left arm, put my left hand into the mail slot . . . held the letter between my tightly clenched fingers . . . and thought.

If I drop this letter in the box, I will open many, many doors. Some of the doors might be better kept closed. Some of them might be very uplifting and fulfilling. If I drop this letter in the box, I will never be able to undo what is going to happen. I must be ready to accept whatever happens.

Elaine's friend said nice things about her. So Elaine was probably a very nice person. Probably. Perhaps she was not nice anymore. Perhaps she'd be offended and take some legal action against me. Perhaps she'd be someone whom I really didn't want to know. Perhaps, I thought, if she's anything like me (and I'm a nice guy, right?), then she'd be the kind of person I wanted to meet. But whatever the result, if I drop the letter, the door will be open. There'll be no turning back. I would be changing her life. I'd be changing my life and hers.

I looked around the post office parking lot. Still no cars were pulling in. I wasn't in the way of anyone.

I sat there with the motor running and with my hand hanging in the drive-up mail slot. Thinking. Thinking. I just had to do it. I couldn't leave here with the letter. I'd come too far for that. Be brave. Say a prayer, and drop it in the box. I said a prayer. I dropped it in the box.

*I dropped the letter in the box!* It made a light sliding-paper sound as it slid into the darkness of the mailbox. It was October 24, 1994, twenty-six years after I'd begun my search. I stared out at the darkness of the night, as dark as the knowledge of what kind of ending there'd be to this new drama I started tonight. And I prayed to God that there'd be no harm done.

I slowly drove away from the post office feeling relieved. I expected to feel scared, but I felt relieved. It was done. Something was going to happen. I had finally done it. Oh boy, had I done it!

I drove home and told my wife. Be ready for anything, she cautioned me. I was ready. I guess I was. Oh well, it had to be done. I couldn't keep this up any more. Now all I had to do was sit and wait.

A week went by. No answer. Nothing. My wife said that I probably scared the hell out of her. "Yeah, that's possible," I reasoned. "But I have the right person." "How so?" she asked.

"Well, if I had sent it to the wrong person, she would have called by now (or would have had someone else call) to ask me what was going on, wonder if I'm some kind of nut, and ask who the hell was I." No calls. Another week.

Yep, my wife figured I scared the living heck out of her. I was confident—confident that something would happen.

Another week and nothing happened. Three weeks now. Pretty soon, I figured. Give her time to think it over. "My letter was well composed," I flattered myself. She'd have no alternative but to give in to my well-chosen and well-reasoned letter.

Exactly four weeks to the day that I mailed it, I came home on afternoon break from teaching school. No one except me was home. I went to the mailbox and idly shuffled through the mail.

There amongst the solicitations for credit card applications and other usual junk was a little greeting-card size, light brown envelope. I turned it over to see whom it was for and looked at a gold return address label *which was from Elaine Lewis* and which had the Elgin Oval address.

My head was swimming. Oh my God! This was the first time that I had touched anything belonging to my birthmother. Was she telling me to hit the road? Hey, I reasoned, she's at least made some form of contact, some form of answer. And there was her own handwriting. I sat at the dining room table and turned the unopened envelope over and over a few times. This is it, my first direct contact with my birthmother. I nervously opened the envelope, took out the little brown stationery, opened it up, and read:

*Dear One:*

*If you are still interested in seeing me, please call me.*

*Will be waiting to hear from you. I can give you instructions how to get out here where I am.*

*God bless you*
*Elaine Lewis*

Success! She had given me her phone number to call. I sat there reflecting. Since no one was home except me, I had peace and quiet. It was early afternoon. And here I was looking at the handwriting of the person who gave birth to me over 50 years ago. This was our first mutual communication. I sat there a while longer reflecting on how far I'd come, the searching, city directories, phone calls, letters, records, the guesses, the wrong addresses, and on and on. And now it was over. Not only that, but the object of my search wanted to meet me. She really wanted to meet me! I sat there reading and re-reading the short note. The only thing I had not uncovered in my long searches was her phone number, and there it was in her note.

Well, no one was at home with me and, what the heck, why not make the big call? I picked up the phone without hesitation, proud of my success, dialed the number; and after a couple rings, a weak little voice answered.

"Hello."
"May I speak to Elaine Lewis?"
"This is Elaine Lewis."

"This is Larry Weeks." I paused to reflect on her voice, the first time I had heard her voice—the first time in my life.

"Hello, Dear," she said. And then we started to talk. She sounded receptive to my few and gentle questions. We started talking about little things at first. She explained that she had had a stroke a few years ago and now has Parkinson's disease. She lives in her trailer with the nephew of her late husband. She needs a cane to get around; but, hey, it could be worse, she said. Yes, she'd love to meet me.

We continued talking. I'm sure we were both trying to figure out what kind of person each of us was. Her risk at answering my letter was great. She hadn't called anyone who had known me. She hadn't known a single thing about me when I called. As far as she knew, I could be a nice guy, a jerk, an alcoholic, an opportunist, a loudmouthed fool, or whatever. She had no way of knowing unless she was able to get a clue or two from my two-page letter to her.

I already knew that Elaine was a nice person, generous to a fault, neat dresser, and opinionated. I already knew that she had had a parrot, cats, liked crossword puzzles, and coffee. I already knew that she was kind of short, had piercing blue eyes, and had had major cancer surgery years ago. Elaine was willing to take the risk of answering my letter.

She then began to explain to me how to get to her trailer. "Then you turn here and drive to there, and then you come to a guard shack and . . . ," I listened for a few moments and then interrupted her: "Elaine, I . . .

I have already been on your street and have seen your trailer."

She paused. "I had a feeling you'd already been here."

She had a few things to tell me when we were face to face. Something about my father. She couldn't tell me over the phone. Her nephew was there right now, and she didn't feel right talking about these sensitive things. "Who was my father?" I don't know why I asked that question. It wasn't really on my mind. But she had brought it up, and I thought I'd toss it out to see what she'd say.

His name was Joseph *Baker*. Joseph *Baker*. *Baker*. *Baker* was the name that Elaine was listed under in the 1946 obituary for her little sister Rita Mary. *Baker*. One mystery cleared up. You were married to Joseph Baker? "No," she said. "We never married. I'll tell you more when you come out." There went the "*loving-married-couple-dying-in-a-car-crash*" story I was told about years ago.

We continued with little questions and little answers. I told her that she had a daughter-in-law and three grandchildren. We talked about all kinds of things. We decided that the following Saturday would be fine for my first visit. How about 11 o'clock in the morning on Saturday? Swell. I couldn't wait. It was now Monday, and all I had to do was wait till Saturday. It seemed like an eternity. But what the heck . . . I waited 26 years . . . I could wait 5 more days.

Since some important details would have to wait until Saturday, we concluded our conversation. I was deeply moved. I sat there with my head swimming. I couldn't believe all that had transpired. I couldn't wait to tell my wife and kids. I called Elaine one more time during that week. I just had to. I couldn't wait until Saturday.

## The Meeting

The week seemed longer than normal. I gathered all the data I had about the *Vincent* family. I would probably leave all the documents in the car when I got to her house. I wouldn't want to scare her. I could save the hundred of pages of information for some other time when we had gotten to know each other better.

I got myself a haircut; her kid should have a haircut, right? My wife bought a nice planter with something in it that had lots of leaves. I don't know plants. All I knew was that it was leafy and green. But it looked like something that Elaine might like.

Since I'm one for arriving at places early, I figured it would take an hour to drive to that side of town. So, just to guarantee that I'd be there on time and not a minute too late, I left my house one and a *half* hours before our meeting time. As luck would have it, the traffic was super; and there I was in her neighborhood a good 45 minutes before we were to meet. I drove past the trailer park and went into the little village of Olmsted Falls just south about a mile or so down the road. I found a little diner and went in.

I sat at the counter; had a cup of coffee; bought a modest breakfast; and, surprisingly, was not a bit nervous. I took out a copy of the letter I'd sent her and read it a few times. Nice letter. Well-written. I took out Elaine's note and read it. Then I read it again. I sat there reflecting on the fact that I was minutes away from meeting the woman who gave birth to me 50 long years ago. I was now right down the street from her. I wondered what she was thinking right now.

Soon it was ten minutes before our meeting time. I was calm. I got back in the car, drove up the road toward the trailer park, turned left into the park's entrance, pulled up to the guard shack and . . . this time when I was asked whom I was there to see, I confidently announced, "*Elaine Lewis.*" "What's her address," the lady asked, trying to see if I was really supposed to be there. *"37 Elgin Oval,"* I replied. With a smile, she ushered me through; and off I went as if I owned the world, driving slowly toward the 26-year destination.

The trees were bare; it was now November 26, 1994, a date and month that would have a big significance later in my story. The trailer park was full of trees and little winding roads. I remember how pretty it was the last time I was here prowling around looking for Elaine's home. Elgin Oval came into view; and there, two trailers from the corner was her home. No station wagon in the driveway. The sun was shining.

I pulled into her driveway. After getting the bag that had the planter from the floor of the back seat, I walked around to a door that was on the south side of the trailer. I went up a couple steps and leaned forward to knock on the screen door. "Come in," I heard a small voice say. "The door's open."

I opened the door; and, before I took a half step into the trailer, a little woman lunged forward and, putting her arms around my waist, said, "Oh, you're so big. God bless you." I put my arms around the woman and hugged her.

I couldn't see her face; all I could see was the top of her very curly, gray-haired head. Then the little woman looked up with wet eyes. I saw those piercing blue eyes I had heard about. I saw a gray-haired lady standing there holding a four-legged metal walking cane, her hand shaking softly.

What she saw as she looked up at me, I can only guess. I was moved. Things seemed to be swirling around me. Twenty-six years of searching were over. Time stood still. I continued looking down at her curly gray hair. Her feelings at this moment appeared to be exactly as mine were. We hugged a little longer.

"I brought you a plant," I said as we stood next to each other. I had to say something. She thanked me. "Please sit down," she motioned, ushering me into the dining area to the right. I looked around at a decent size trailer, neat looking and bright. The kitchen table was cleaned off, and a cup and saucer were there waiting for me to have some coffee.

She had a stack of picture albums on the corner of the kitchen table. "Let me show you some of your relatives," she said. Her voice was small; her gait was smaller. Her hand shook softly. She scooted around the table with tiny, slow, measured steps. And off we went for almost an hour, staring at each other, talking to each other, and acting as though we'd both done a good thing. We were nervous, admittedly.

Many of the pictures that she showed me of her brothers indicated to me that there was a strong resemblance between them and me for sure. And one of the pictures of her, taken when she was about 19 years old, completely overwhelmed me[7]. She looked absolutely beautiful with long hair and the young striking face of a young woman who, a few years later, would be deciding whether or not to give up her first and only child.

    We continued with small talk. Fifty years of catching up. I was determined to convince her that she made a good decision when she opened the door for our reunion. She walked with a metal cane that had four little feet. She hobbled from point to point. She laughed a lot. She had a twinkle in her eye. She was full of stories to tell. Some were happy. Most were not.

---

[7] The photo is on the cover of this manuscript

## Elaine's Story

Her parents, Frederick and Alvina, had ten children. I knew of only nine. Her father was not around much. One of her sisters, Shirley, the third child of this marriage, died three months after birth. That's why there was no mention of a surviving sister Shirley in the obituaries. A couple of Elaine's brothers had already died. Three brothers were still alive. All of her sisters were dead.

Her father did not play a big part in her life, although she had kind things to say of him. Apparently, her father—my grandfather—had been an alcoholic and had seldom been around their home as they grew up. Her mother—my grandmother—had basically raised all ten children.

My maternal grandfather, Frederick Vincent, died about four years before I was born (1940). He had been a heavy drinker, and it is reported that his death was the result of complications from drinking.[8]

Elaine had been happily engaged to a young man who was going into the service during the war. He broke off the engagement before he shipped out. She was willing to wait for him, but he didn't want her to wait for him. She was crushed. Soon after this depressing event, she, her sister, and widowed mother met three soldiers at Fort Snelling near St. Paul. One of them, Joseph Baker, swept her off her feet. He was a few years her senior and was soon to be mustered out

---

[8] information from *Background Information:* Prepared for Larry Weeks, Catholic Charities Service letter, August 9, 2000.

of the army. Come to Cleveland with him, he invited, and they'd settle down. He had a brother and sister already there, so things would be all right.

Since she was on the rebound, and since she was ready to spread her wings, she left St. Paul on a bus with Joseph Baker, came to Cleveland, and settled down. Her family back in St. Paul had met Joseph and had assumed that they had gotten married when they got to Cleveland. But they had not married. Never did. Since her family thought she had married Joseph, Elaine was listed in her sister Rita Mary's obituary as *Mrs. Elaine Baker*.

But once she got to Cleveland, she became aware that Joseph was not all she'd thought he was. It was obvious that he was not going to be a good provider. His work was infrequent, and his drinking excessive. He played a bass fiddle in a band somewhere in Cleveland and spent or drank the money before he got home.

One day in September of 1943 Elaine became pregnant. Joseph's brother asked Elaine if she knew that Joseph was already married and did she know that Joseph had a daughter. Elaine said Joseph told her he was divorced, but he wasn't.

Now she was pregnant by a married man, living in a 4th-floor walk-up sleeping room, was the only one earning a regular paycheck, was many miles from home, and had no one to turn to. Her situation back home with her mother was not the best. Her mother, who had become a widow about four years earlier, had her own problems with a number of minor children still at home. If she went home pregnant, her mother would give her the old "*You make your bed, lie in it*" song and dance, so Elaine thought. She couldn't go home to admit defeat.

After much soul searching and being aware of what society felt toward single, unwed mothers, and eager to give her baby a chance to be raised in a decent home, she decided to give me up for adoption. She waited until two days before my birth to go to the Cleveland Catholic Charities to tell them of her decision. They suggested that she go back home to St. Paul. They were willing to pay her train fare to go back, but she declined. She had made up her mind.

According to Catholic Charities, Elaine came to Cleveland with my father who promised to marry her when they arrived. But, supposedly, when he learned of her pregnancy, he stated he would marry her only if she would agree to being married by a Justice of the Peace. In the meantime, Elaine learned that my father was a heavy drinker and was not very responsible, having held five or six different jobs. She then felt he was not the kind of person she wanted to marry. My father then left town refusing to help her with expenses unless she would marry him and told her how to contact him if she decided to marry him as she wished. How he intended to do this since he was still married was unclear.[9]

On Thursday, June 15, at 5:10 p.m., after a full-term pregnancy and eight hours of labor, I was born. I

---

[9] information from *Background Information:* Prepared for Larry Weeks, Catholic Charities Service letter, August 9, 2000.

was immediately removed from her presence and put in an orphan nursery. Because Elaine had no money nor any means to pay her bill, the nuns made her work off her hospital bill by living in a dormitory and doing various chores for four or five months. During that time, she lived with other young ladies in the same situation.

Then, one day, a few months later, after paying her dues, Elaine opened the door of the hospital, walked out the door, and disappeared from my life. I was transferred soon after to the St. Vincent De Paul orphanage where I was to stay until I was three or four; I would be then transferred to Parmadale, the large orphanage on Cleveland's southwest side. She said that Joseph pestered her for a few years and then completely disappeared. I could tell from her tone of voice that she didn't have too much good to say about him. Finding information about Joseph would be difficult.

Elaine then went on with her life. She roomed with a couple families over the next 19 years, eventually marrying the brother-in-law of one of the family heads. I already knew that. I also knew all the addresses where she lived. I also knew where she had worked and what she did there.

In 1963 she married James E. Lewis, which explained why she disappeared from the city directory. A few years later, she had a radical mastectomy. Her husband was very supportive and gave her the love and encouragement she needed. Nine years after they married, the only real true love of her life, one of the few good men she had met in her life, died of a stroke as she was holding him.

So, in 1972 James Lewis was buried at the cemetery I had visited. Elaine stayed in the house they owned, but she had to work two jobs to keep up the mortgage. It was shortly after James' death and her working two jobs that she got a call from her former coworker that somebody was trying to find her because he thought she was his mother. Not being in any frame of mind to affirm such an accusation, she vigorously denied the claim. And she went on with her life.

Following a stroke, which she felt was due to her working two jobs, she sold the home that James and she had lived in and bought a trailer. Then a nephew of her late husband moved in with her and gave her companionship and helped with things she could not do on her own.

In the fall of 1994, while visiting the cemetery where James had been buried, she saw an artificial flower pushed into the ground in front of her husband's headstone. She had no idea where it had come from. She had no idea that it was I who put it there.

One day in October of 1994, while going sifting through the letters that were in her mailbox, she found a № 10 business envelope with a return address that was unfamiliar to her. Then she opened the letter and began to read the letter I sent. She was shocked. No one knew about her being pregnant and giving up a baby except for her late husband. She had told him about having baby years ago. But no one else knew— not her coworkers, friends, nor any relatives. But somehow there were rumors among some of her in-laws about the "love child" she had years before. There were only two people alive who knew the secret for sure. One of the people was reading my letter, and the other person had written the letter.

    Elaine said she was furious. Her secret was staring at her in front of her face. She read and re-read the letter. She folded it up. What if her late husband's nephew Lester found it? Lester lived in the trailer and helped take care of her. She tore off both the letterhead and the signature part of the letter. She folded, unfolded, read, and refolded the letter. She read it over and over again. "Anyone who went through all the trouble that he did to find me should be given a chance to meet me," she reasoned. "Whoever this guy was certainly was insistent and knew how to write a letter." She thought and thought. And then she took out her brown stationery and wrote the letter to her only son and child whom she had not seen since birth.

* * *

    But I was happy. The Good Lord had allowed me to meet my birthmother before either of us had died. She was sharp minded and quick witted. What she lacked in physical abilities, she made up for with humor and smiles. We had talked about many things. She asked me if I liked football. Sure. Well, Notre Dame's on the tube. OK, let's watch the football game. "Want a beer?" "Sure." "Get me one too," she said. So here I was, fifty years after my birth, popping the top on two beers, munching chips, and watching Notre Dame college football with Elaine. Mission accomplished!

I left her home very glad. I felt that I had made someone very happy. I was happy too, no question about that. But I had this feeling that I had done something very special for a little lady who years before had made a tough decision to give up the only baby she had in order to allow him to have a home and a family.

At the time of our first meeting, Elaine had three surviving brothers, Earl who lived in St. Paul, Eugene, and Jerome (Pal) who stayed in Florida during the winter with their wives.

Gene and Pal would drive through Cleveland when they left St. Paul and again when they returned to St. Paul. On each drive through Cleveland, they'd stop to visit Elaine. She told each of her two brothers in Florida that she had a surprise for them when they visited her the next spring. She wouldn't tell them what it was. "Did you get a new cat?" asked her one brother. "No," she answered. "You'll just have to wait till you get here."

When Eugene drove back to Cleveland, she had me come by the next day to meet my new uncle. She said that he was amazed and very happy to have heard about a new nephew and told her how sorry he felt for her that she had to keep that secret all these years.

When her youngest brother Pal came back and was told about his new nephew, he was not too pleased. He was happy to a certain degree that we were reunited, but he was mad at her for not having come back to St. Paul those many years ago to rejoin the Vincent family.

"Hey, Mom raised ten kids almost by herself, so one more wouldn't have hurt."

"But," Elaine retorted, "my mother told me that if you make your bed, you lie in it." Apparently, Elaine didn't think she could face her mother after leaving St. Paul in one year and returning the next year pregnant. However, I felt that her brother Pal was right.

Every so often I see talk shows where people are reunited after decades and decades of separation. And it is almost impossible for me to watch these reunions without getting very misty eyed.

Yep, I've been there. Elaine and I have already done that. After 50 years we were reunited. We didn't share it on a national television show in front of millions of people, but we had our reunion nonetheless. How can these people share such a moment with the world?

But what's the big deal? What in the world can biological family members have in common after decades of separation? Why do siblings separated at infancy, who are now in their forties, hug each other so passionately after a forty-year reunion?

They don't remember much or anything about each other. They would pass each other on the street under any other circumstances. What's so special about someone saying that this is your brother whom you have never met? Why such a firm and long hug?

How could a mother and child have any reason to hug and cry after a reunion of fifty years? What is there that makes such moments so unique? What creates and fuels such an urge to reunite with a mother, father, brother, or sister whom you've never met? And why do some people in the same situation shrink from a chance to reunite with their own blood relatives?

Something drove me to start and continue the search. Something urged me on. Something made me push closer and closer through a whole series of closed doors. Something made me turn the knob on each closed door. And now the long 26-year search for Elaine was over.

## But Where Was Joseph?

Obviously with my inquisitive nature, my search was not over. I had been very successful finding Elaine and had been warmly accepted by her family. Since there were so many new relatives writing to welcome me and to ask me how I found Elaine, I hastily put together the first part of this manuscript, spell-checked it, proofread it, and then sent copies out. The reactions were unanimous: they were moved by my efforts. They were amazed that Elaine had kept this secret for so many years. They were impressed with my tenacity. All in all, they liked the story I had written and passed it around to other family members.

A couple of my newly acquired relatives wanted to know what else I had known about Joseph Baker. And I had to tell them the same thing: relatively nothing. Elaine had either forgotten a lot about him or didn't want to tell me anything more than basic information.

So, after a couple years of relaxing my search and enjoying the relationship I had with Elaine and her family, I felt it was time for me to press on to find out what I could about Joseph Baker. Who was this man who had entered Elaine's life many years ago and who had left her so quickly?

Basically, from Elaine I knew that his name was Joseph Baker (no middle name that she knew of) and that he was considerably older than she (possibly thirteen years, she said). He was a drinker, a musician (bass fiddle), had a sister Freda and a brother Carl, and that he and his family were from Huntington, West Virginia.

From Catholic Charities, I was told:

*<u>Biological Father:</u> He was not known to the Agency. He had been in Service and was described as being in his early 30s and was of German heritage. It was stated that he had musical talent. He resided in his parental home.*

*These young people had met at an Army Camp. They have considered marriage but could not do so because of the fact that the biological father had been married previously.*

No amount of prying could get any more from Elaine. I would occasionally ask her questions about this smattering of information, but she never divulged anything new. I concluded that he must have been very secretive about his past.

What to do? Since I had had such good luck with city directories here in Cleveland, I figured I'd see if I could do the same with Huntington, West Virginia's directories. I had already searched for Joseph Baker in the Cleveland directories with no results; without a middle name, there was no way to narrow it down to the right one.

There were as many as twenty Joseph Bakers in Cleveland in the 1940s. There were a couple Carl Bakers here and there, but no common addresses that would link the two. A search through the Cleveland Public Library's necrology department would be fruitless. If he were dead, I didn't know when he died; and I had no middle name to make that final link. Even a check with the old Cleveland phone books was useless: a lot of people didn't have phones back then, and there were a billion Joseph Bakers listed.

As a long shot, I wrote to the Huntington Public Library and asked if the reference department had files like the Cleveland Public Library had: obituaries on microfilm, old city directories, and other vital documents of that nature. One of the librarians who specialize in just such information contacted me and told me that the obituaries themselves were not on microfilm, and that she would have to search through daily newspapers for obituaries. So, unless I had a date of death, she'd have to go through each and every newspaper all the way back to the 1940s. And, I didn't even know if Joseph was dead. And, besides, what made me think that Joseph had even returned to Huntington before he died? He could have died in Bug Tussle, Idaho, for all I knew.

If Joseph were really from Huntington, then I reasoned that before he enlisted (or was drafted) into the army, he might have been listed in city directories in the late 1930s and early 1940s. My contact in Huntington mailed me the Baker listings from the 1935 and 1940 city directories which revealed nothing of any interest except that I did find a "Carl P." married to an Edith listed just as I had found a "Carl P." married to an Edith listed in Cleveland's 1943-44 city directory. Therefore, I reasoned, if there were other Bakers listed around Carl's address in Huntington, then I might be able to zero in on uncles, grandfathers, aunts, or whatever. Any address close to Carl's would be suspect. But—no Joseph Baker. The elusive Joseph was hiding down there as he was in Cleveland.

Elaine, my mother, was listed in the 1943-44 Cleveland directory. I thought it odd that Joseph was not listed. Why would she be listed but not he? So, nothing of value was in the Huntington city directories except that I had at least zeroed in on Joseph's brother Carl. Elaine told me that Carl and Edith had divorced, and Carl had then married a woman many years his junior whose name was Myrtle. The 1947 Cleveland city directory had two listings for Carl:

*Carl P. Baker (mach oper) and Edith, 8807 Lorain Ave, Apt 2*
*Carl Baker (driver) and Myrtle, 5013 Prospect Ave.*

But no Joseph Baker. Where was Joseph?

## The Obituary

One day in April of 1996, I came home from work, opened the mailbox, and found an envelope from the Huntington Public Library. I hadn't heard from them for a long time, so I was more than curious.

*Dear Mr. Weeks,*
 *I know you must be thinking it is about time I heard something. Joseph H. Baker is the only Joseph Baker that died in Cabell Co. His obit is included. Information on his death record said he was the son of Albert Baker and Nell Hayes. He was divorced and died of cancer.*
 *I have found nothing on Carl or Karl. Freda Mae Baker married Arthur Hundley, Jr., of Kanawa Co. in 1936 (Book 5, page 142).*

The January 22, 1990, obituary that the librarian enclosed read:

**JOSEPH HOMER BAKER**, *76, of 101-8th Ave., Huntington, died Sunday in Cabell Huntington Hospital. He was a retired civil engineer and musician. Surviving are a daughter Norma Nell Baker of Stevens, Fla.; and a son, Terry Joe Baker, of Huntington. A memorial service will be conducted later. Ferrell Mortuary, Huntington, is in charge of arrangements.*

Now I had something. But *Homer?* His middle name was *Homer?* That could prove to be useful, but I couldn't find any Joseph "H" Bakers in any of the materials I had collected yet. And now I knew who Joseph's daughter was that Elaine said he had. And her name was Norma Nell. And now I also knew I had a half-brother named Terry Joe. Did they know about me? Where were they?

So, I had a half-sister and brother out there somewhere. And they were alive and well just six years ago. If I tried to find them and actually did find them, would I hurt them? Maybe Joseph moved back to Huntington, settled down, and became a wonderful dad to these two kids. Maybe not. Maybe if I were to be able to find his brother or sister, Carl or Freda, I'd be able to introduce myself to them, find out if they remember the drama back in the 1940s (Elaine said they both knew), and then determine if I had a chance to meet either of them or my half-brother or half-sister.

A couple days later, I went to the Latter Day Saints History Center and genealogy library in neighboring Kirtland, Ohio, and started looking for Joseph Homer Baker. If you (1) were dead and (2) had ever received a social security check, then your name, social security number, and a couple other items of interest can be found on either one of two CD-ROMs that are available in most libraries.[10]

A search for Joseph on these CDs proved fruitless. I wasn't sure when he was born. Elaine said he

---

[10] update: Nowadays this Social Security Death Index is available on the internet.

was about 13 years older or so, but still nothing came up on the screen for anyone who would have been old enough or who was born or had died in West Virginia. So, there I sat. Maybe he had never received a social security check. Just for laughs, what if I looked under *Homer*, his middle name.

Bingo! There in front of me was a Homer Baker who showed a death date that was identical to the one on the obituary mailed to me from Huntington. *Homer?* No wonder I couldn't find anything on Joseph Baker. For some reason, he applied for social security under his middle name. But why? The CD showed the following items:

> <u>Homer Baker</u>, *born: December 4, 1913, in Huntington, WV; died: January 21, 1990; social security #234-18-5458*

So, Elaine's memories of his being 13 years or so older than she were wrong; he was only 9 years older. But where did the name *Homer* come from?

In January of 1996, I bought a computer with a CD-ROM player. So I decided to send away for Parson Technology's *Directory USA*, which consisted of two CD-ROMs containing all of the home telephone numbers for everyone in the U.S.A. with a listed home phone. It was amazing to think of all that on two little disks, but I figured I'd search for Terry Joe and Norma Nell. No current listing appeared for Terry Joe in Huntington or anywhere else in West Virginia. In Joseph Baker's obituary, Norma Nell had been listed without a married name, so I assumed that she was still Norma Nell Baker of *Stevens,* Florida. After all, why would obituaries have wrong information? But, there was no such city anywhere in Florida called *Stevens*[11]. So my CD-ROM search proved to be fruitless.

Obviously, this was driving me nuts. I had a lot of information from a genealogical standpoint, and here I was 300 miles away from lots of good primary sources. What to do? After stewing over this for a month or so, I decided to make a trip to Huntington, some 250 miles away.

I called the librarian and told her I was coming down to spend a day in her library. She said she'd rustle up whatever she could find while I was on the way. So I gathered all my data, packed my jammies and tooth-brush, took enough money for one night's stay, loaded up with some sandwiches and pop in an ice-filled cooler, kissed my wife goodbye, and headed south.

---

[11] Norma Nell Baker of Stevens, Florida was really Norma Nell Stevens of Florida

## My Trip to Huntington

I left at 5 a.m. on a Friday morning and sped down I-77. After a couple stops here and there, I wound up five hours later at the Huntington Public Library. Up to the second floor I went, and soon I was busy chatting with the lady who had done a lot of searching for me. She had a gift waiting for me: my biological grandfather's September 29, 1971, obituary complete with his photo:

> ***ALBERT W. BAKER***, *85, of 2752 Guyan Ave., died Wednesday in a Huntington hospital. Funeral services will be conducted Saturday at 2 p.m. at the Trinity Church of God, of which he was a member, by the Rev. Fred Davey. Burial will be in Ridgelawn Memorial Park. Born July 8, 1886, in Lincoln County, he was a son of the late Moss and Nancy Warrick Baker. He was a retired engineer for the Owens-Illinois, Inc., Glass Container Division plant. A brother Lawrence Baker, preceded him in death. He was a member of Mohawk Tribe 11, Improved Order of Red Men*[12]. *Survivors include the widow, Mrs. Nell Hayes Baker; three sons, Carl P. Baker of Tucson, Ariz., and Homer and Thomas G. Baker of Huntington; a*

---

[12] This is a social organization similar to the Y.M.C.A.'s Indian Scout program. There is no affiliation with any American Indian tribes.

*daughter, Mrs. Freda Yuckes[13] of Cleveland, Ohio; two brothers, Charles Baker of Easy Lynn and William F. Baker of Wilmington, N.C., 12 grandchildren and several great-grandchildren. Friends may call at the Beard Mortuary after 4 p.m. Friday. The body will be taken to the church an hour before the services.*

Finding a neat, quiet little corner in the genealogy department, I began digging through the Huntington city directories starting from 1990 (the year of Joseph's death) and went back as far as I could. Along the way, I stumbled over Terry Joe's name and address here and there. I was able to find a Norma N., but no Norma Nell in any of the city directories.

The 1986 through 1990 city directories showed:

*Baker, Joseph, retd* [14], *h101 8th Ave, Apt 605, 525-6706*

The 1985 city directory showed:

*Baker, Joseph, retd, h54a, 6th Ave W, 525-6706*

The 1984 city directory showed:

*Baker, Joseph, retd, h542, 6th Ave W, Apt. 2, 525-6706*

---

[13] YUCKSTAS. Don't necessarily trust obituaries.
[14] *retd* is an abbreviation for *retired*

Joseph was not listed in the 1981 through 1983 directories.

The 1980 city directory showed:
*Baker, Joseph, retd, h425 5th Ave., Apt 1b*

He disappeared until the 1971 city directory:
*Baker, Joseph H (Reva F) retd, h214 6th Ave*

To sum it up, it appeared that Joseph was never in one spot too long; and in some cases, he wasn't anywhere that the city directory noted. My illusions that maybe he had settled down with his two children were a bit shaky considering all this movement. But I did stumble over a Reva F. Baker who undoubtedly was another wife. Oy!

The librarian took me next door to the city hall and helped me get Joseph's death certificate where it was noted that his name was Joseph Homer Baker; but to the left of his typed name, some one had handwritten *HOMER*. It said he died January 21, 1990, at the age of 76. He was born on December 4, 1913, in Branchland, West Virginia. His final occupation was listed as *civil engineer,* and his final residence was listed (which I already had). He apparently was immediately cremated in Portsmouth, Ohio. Immediate cause of death was *"due to cardio respiratory arrest, due to small-cell carcinoma, due to sepsis[15]."*

---

[15] **sepsis:** a toxic condition resulting from the spread of bacteria or their products from a focus of infection

While I was glancing through the city hall's records, I discovered a record of a marriage license being issued on September 6, 1941, to *Mr. Homer Baker, Lincoln County, Barboursville, and Miss Helen Louise Plymale.* The record showed they were married a week later on September 13, 1941. So, Joseph looked like he had been a busy guy. I reckoned that this Helen Plymale was the mother of the little girl that Elaine was told about back in 1944. Then he apparently had an affair with my biological mother. Then the city directory showed him married to a *Reva F.* back in 1971. And it looked like he was divorced when he died.

That night I got myself a room at a *Red Roof Inn* and tried to digest all the information I had gleaned that day. I had a large map of Huntington, so I spread it out on the motel room table, and tried to find and highlight all the addresses I had found that day. Between Joseph and his son Terry Joe, I had quite a few highlighted spots on the map. Knowing that I had to leave the next day by noon, I tried to figure out what information I did NOT have. And, of course, how much more could I possibly get without overkill.

There was no Terry Joe Baker nor Norma Nell Baker listed in the 1996 phone book, so it wouldn't have been possible to contact anyone. Besides, what if they didn't know anything about me? I didn't want to hurt anyone. I figured I could drive home, pour over the information, and decide what to do next. I did, however, want to visit the last address where Joseph lived in 1990. So, before the library would open the next day, I decided to see if I could find Joseph's last home.

Early the next morning, after a pensive breakfast at the *Omelet Shoppe* on Rte. 60, I got out my map and drove to Joseph's last address: 101-8th Avenue, Apt. 605. Without too much difficulty, I found the tall, handsome high-rise that he called home for the last few years of his life. I pulled into the semicircular front drive, stopped, and thought for a while. Was this an apartment house, hospital, or old age home? Something told me to turn off the engine and go inside.

I found a lobby with a locked glass door, buttons, and names on the wall. The front door would not open without someone buzzing you in. A few old folks were sitting in a lobby just a few feet from the front door. I tapped my ring on the glass door and got a lady's attention.

She slowly opened the door and asked if she could help me. "Well," I asked, "is this a hospital, or what is it?"

"This is a retirement home," she answered. She sounded like she'd be receptive to more questioning.

"Ma'am. I wonder if you would help me. I'm looking for anyone who might remember someone who I believe was my father. I just drove down from Cleveland to see what I could find out about him. I've never met him; but from what I've learned, he lived in this building when he died." I spoke as sincerely as I could.

"I've been here quite a few years. Who was he?" She asked.

"Joseph Baker."

Instantly she answered, "Oh yes. I knew him. I lived in the apartment directly over his. He liked his booze, ya' know," she leaned over to tell me with a twinkle in her eye. "Yeah, he lived here when he died. Real nice man. His son T.J. would come and stay with him once in a while for a week or two. Yeah, I remember him. You're who?" she asked.

"As far as I know, I'm his son, Ma'am. Problem is, I don't think that either of his children knows I exist. So, I'm kinda' going at this slowly." The fact that she called Terry Joe *T.J.* further convinced me that I had the right Joseph Baker.

"Do you know anyone who knows T.J.?" I asked.

She paused. "Yes."

"Well, here's my business card with my home phone number on it. If you could get this to T.J., I'd appreciate it." She looked down at the card, looked back up at me as if maybe I shouldn't want to meet T.J., and said she'd get the card to him.

I was puzzled by her look, but I returned to my car happy to know that apparently I was very, very close to knowing all I'd need to know. Maybe too close.

I went back to the Huntington Library, checked out a few loose ends, said goodbye to my librarian friend, started up my car, and drove home full of thoughts and content in the knowledge that something was going to break.

### Well Then, Who Am I?

The following Monday, early in my workday, my office phone rang. A male voice with a Southern accent was on the other end. The old lady at the retirement home had contacted a girl whom Terry Joe had dated and who told him about my visit. He pleasantly asked me what I looked like, how tall was I, what color hair I had, and on and on.

Then, after about five minutes of our introductory exchange, he asked, "Do you have a hundred dollars you don't need?"

"What?"

"Do you have a hundred dollars I could have?"

Oh, my God, I thought to myself. "No, not really." What did I just do? What kind of can of worms did I just open? Now I knew why the little old lady at the nursing home looked at me so hesitantly when I asked her to link me up with T.J.

Instantly he changed the subject. "Boy, oh boy, wait till Norma Nell finds out about you. I'll call her today and give her your phone number." Great, I thought. I wonder what she'll want, my corneas, one of my kidneys, perhaps my liver. Then he started talking about Joe Homer Baker's life up in Cleveland years back. Not only did he know about our father's romance up north with Elaine, but T.J. also added a twist to what he knew. "You got me confused now, Larry," he said. "From what I was told years ago, the boy Dad had in Cleveland was run over by a bus or something. We got a picture somewhere of a little boy in a coffin that I guess Dad brought home with him. It's an actual photo of his kid in a coffin. So, if that's Dad's kid, then who are you?"

Fair question. But I knew that I was Elaine's boy. And she told me that Joseph was my father. I didn't know anything about any little boy, especially not in a coffin. "Anyway, Larry, my sister Norma Nell will be thrilled to hear that she has another brother. This is great. Hey, OK if I have her call you? She can probably tell you more about that photo."

"Sure, whatever!" I answered, happy to know that my half-brother had accepted me but truly concerned about his casual request for money from a complete stranger.

The next day I got another phone call from the sweetest sounding young lady, my half-sister Norma Nell. Wow! She had another brother, she exclaimed!

"My daughter Wendy said Terry Joe called to say that we had a brother up in Cleveland, some kind of big shot." (I wasn't really a big shot, but to someone who tries to borrow money from a complete stranger, maybe I really WAS a big shot.)

She chatted on and on and was just absolutely delightful to listen to. I didn't hear half of what she said; I was too busy enjoying her excitement and Southern accent. And then she interrupted, "Larry, be honest with me. Did Terry try to borrow money from you?"

"No," I fibbed and nervously changed the subject.

"C'mon," she interrupted. "He DID try to borrow money, didn't he?"

I kind of stammered on a bit, and again Norma interrupted me.

"How much?"

Weakly, I said, "A hundred bucks," and tried to continue our conversation.

Norma let out a scream over the phone. "Oh, no! I don't believe he did that. We're not like that!" she entreated.

"Really?" I thought. "Terry Joe is like that!" Norma apologized profusely, telling me that Terry has had behavior problems and has always been kind of an outcast in the family. I felt relieved that my money and body parts were safe. I still wondered, though, if Terry was going to drive up here to Mentor, Ohio, park on our front lawn, and live in his car.

Yeah, she remembered the story about the little boy up in Cleveland, and remembered having seen the photo of the kid in the coffin when she was very little. Therefore, although she knew Joseph had had an affair and that he and his girlfriend gave the newborn to a hunchbacked landlady, the Baker family was confident that the chapter was closed with the death of the little kid. Therefore, who was I?

I assured her that I was alive and well and that I didn't know anything about some kid in a coffin. From what my mother Elaine had told me, she chased Joseph out of her life after she had given me up at birth, and that was that.

Norma Nell told me that Joseph Baker's real first name was *Homer*. For some reason, his father (our grandfather—or *pappaw* as they're called in West Virginia) named him Homer and gave him no middle name. Joseph couldn't stand the name *Homer*, so he arbitrarily picked the name Joseph and used it until most people thought that that was his real name.

Joseph, she continued, was married six times to a total of five wives (one of whom he married twice—Norma and Terry's mom). Norma told me that Joe and his first wife Frances had a little girl named Betty Jo. Joseph, it turned out, was not much of a provider. Norma had been in touch with Betty Jo right up to Joseph's death in 1990, but somehow there was an argument among the siblings at the hospital that caused Betty Jo to sever contact with Norma Nell and her brother Terry Joe.

Joe and his next wife, Helen Plymale, had a daughter JoAnn. Again, Joseph was not a good provider. After they divorced, Helen remarried, and her new husband adopted JoAnn. Norma had successfully found her during a sibling search early in 1996, but apparently JoAnn was apprehensive about establishing any relationship with the Bakers.

Of course, there was the affair with Elaine, and quite possibly, I reasoned, another affair with the mother of whoever the boy was in the coffin.

Joseph then married Genevieve Egnor around 1950 and had Terry Joe in 1950 and then Norma Nell in January of 1953. She said that Joseph contributed next to nothing to their financial upkeep, but would come over to baby-sit for her and her brother when their mom went to work at the local glass factory across the Ohio River from Chesapeake, Ohio, in Huntington. Joseph and Genevieve were married to each other twice. Genevieve died in 1991, a year after Joseph.

And there were a couple more wives and a few more divorces and on and on. His drinking, Norma Nell said, made it next to impossible for him to hold down a job for any length of time. Although he was kind and gentle to the children, he really didn't play much of a role at all in their upbringing or development.

Then one day Norma and her husband Lyle returned from Washington, D.C., to hear her daughter Wendy buzzing with excitement that Terry Joe had called Wendy the night before. He wanted to tell Norma that he had talked to someone up in Cleveland who claimed to be their dad's kid. Norma had just gone through some recent soul searching and was distressed that she never had a sibling with whom she was close. Wouldn't it be nice to have had a brother that she could relate to and whom she could actually call "brother"? Terry Joe was not that person. She'd had too many problems with Terry Joe during her lifetime. And now she came home from Washington and heard that she had another brother? She couldn't wait to find out what was going on up there in Cleveland.

Although Joseph was not coming across too well in my thoughts, it was just a thrill talking to this lovely sounding woman who was very excited about having stumbled across a new brother. She promised to get me in touch with Thomas and Christalie Baker, Joseph's only surviving brother and sister-in-law.

And, true to her word, the news of Joseph's unknown child traveled through the Baker family. Thomas and Christalie contacted me within days and told me that they, in fact, had met Elaine many, many years ago and remembered how pretty she was. But they too had seen the photo of the kid in the coffin. So who was this kid? Did Joseph make him up? If so, where did the photograph come from? And who had that picture? Maybe there was something written on the back of that photo that would give a clue. They seemed as excited and as warm as Norma Nell. I was happy that I had apparently done a nice thing by this accidental entry into the Baker family.

Two biological cousins soon contacted me: Thomas' son, Larry Allen, and Roy Baker, the son of Roy Lee who died in 1943. Both of them were very warm and welcomed me into the Baker clan. They were interested in who I was; what I was doing; when I'd be able to visit them; and, of course, if I'm alive (and I am), then who was the little boy in the coffin?

Cousin Roy said he remembered as a child being spooked about even picking up the photo album at his grandmother's house because he knew there was some dead kid's picture in it. No, they didn't know where the photo was. They were now intrigued by the mystery I had brought to the Baker family. Joseph must have had two affairs in Cleveland way back then, one of which was apparently unknown to his family back home. And maybe showing this photo around was his way of accounting for the one child that they DID know about. But where would Joseph get a photo of a dead kid in a coffin?

## Huntington's Aftermath

Originally this story ended with my discovery of and successful reunion with Elaine. And that's where I thought it should end. Little did I suspect that I would ever discover the information about Joseph that I uncovered in a few short weeks. Had it just been a few welcomes and handshakes, I might not have felt that I needed to add to this story. But read on. You will be surprised.

I wrestled with the idea of telling Elaine about all the stuff I had unearthed about Joseph. I didn't want to hurt her. It was obvious that Joseph had caused her a lot of grief many, many years ago. But I also knew that she probably figured that if I pursued a 26-year search to find her, why wouldn't I want to know about my father, too? And she really didn't give me too much to go on: Joseph Baker, from Huntington, 13 years or so older than she, no middle name, had a brother Carl and a sister Freda, played the bass fiddle in a jazz band, and was a heavy drinker. Not much to go on. But as you've read, I found out a whole bunch with just a little to work with. Should I tell her or not? If I tell her a few things that I recently learned, maybe that will jog her memory. I decided to go softly. All I had to do was look into Elaine's intense blue eyes to see that she was a very sensitive person.

During one of our weekly phone calls, I decided to tell Elaine that, on a whim, I wrote to the Huntington Library and asked if they could come up with an obituary for Joseph Baker. And then I told her that after a year's search (it actually *did* take that long to get it) the library sent me the Joseph Homer Baker obituary.

Elaine didn't seem alarmed or surprised. She was mildly curious about Joseph's demise anyway. Well, I told her, the librarian said he died of cancer in 1990. She didn't comment. The obituary mentions two children, a girl and a boy. Well, she knew of one little girl, she said. Didn't know of the boy (she was actually referring to his daughter JoAnn from Joe's second marriage—not these two subsequent children). And now that I mentioned it, she DID remember Joseph telling her his middle name was Homer. I told her that Joe was only nine years older than she, not thirteen or so as she'd surmised.

"What else did you learn?" she queried. I told her that the librarian was thrilled that I had gotten in contact with the siblings in the obituary, and that Norma Nell was thrilled to hear of a new brother. And not only that, Elaine, I continued, Norma Nell and the rest of my new half-siblings and cousins are in a deep quandary over a photo of a dead boy in a coffin.

I told her that Joseph came back to Huntington and told his family that he and Elaine had had a little boy and had given the boy to their hunchbacked landlady to raise. Nope, Elaine said. Never heard anything about that—I only had one child. He must have had a baby from some other girl friend, Elaine offered.

Well, I continued, a couple of the Bakers remember having met you in Huntington years ago. Elaine said she couldn't remember ever having gone to

Huntington. Anyway, I continued, they've all been super about their new relative—me—and have welcomed me graciously. Elaine said she was happy for me.

During the next few weeks she would occasionally ask me if I'd heard anything else. Nothing new, I told her. I had mailed tons of family tree research sheets to a couple cousins and uncles and was awaiting their updates. But the story of a kid in a coffin still was coming up.

And, I added, in early August of 1996, I was going to have the honor of meeting my half-sister for the first time. Elaine said she'd love to meet her if she ever came up to Cleveland. And during the next few weeks, she told me she thought she remembered having visited Huntington once a long time ago. Now it was all coming back, she said.

Then one day she told me over the phone that she had something to tell me, something that she had to tell me in person. I would have to wait until I came over to visit her to find out. Not hazarding a guess, and not necessarily connecting her secrecy to the kid in the coffin, I waited until the following Sunday, drove over to her home, exchanged the usual welcome hug, helped her into the dinette, and with big blue eyes, now again wet with tears, and a small weak voice, she began to tell me a story.

## The Kid in the Coffin

In 1944, knowing that she was pregnant and that Joseph Baker was not going to be a good provider, she decided to give me up for adoption. The Catholic Charity officials wanted to send her back to St. Paul since she had no one here who could help her. She had no friends or relatives anywhere around Cleveland. Joseph knew she'd decided to give up the baby. She was also too far-gone to send home to St. Paul; she delivered me two days later.

Following my birth, she stayed at the *Loretta Home*, a special home for mothers who were about to deliver or who had very recently delivered their soon-to-be-given-away babies. In order to pay off their medical bills, the women had to stay there for four or five months; do menial chores around the home and hospital; help the nuns; and in general, try to get their acts together and pay back the hospital before they returned to the real world.

Since Elaine was a favorite of the nuns, they would let her leave the building every so often to buy gum, candy, or whatever the other women needed. During these trips to the corner store, Elaine said, she would occasionally rendezvous with Joseph Baker.

Joe wanted her back and promised that, once she got out, he would prove to her that he was a changed man. She had nowhere to go, no friends or family in Cleveland, so she reconsidered; and, when she left the Loretta Home, she gave Joseph another chance.

They moved into a small rooming house on Prospect Avenue in Cleveland's near east side whose landlady, Ethel Cash, was a hunchback. Because of her deformity, Elaine was told that Ethyl could not have children. The Homer Baker/Elaine Vincent romance rekindled; and early in 1945, Elaine was again pregnant with Joseph's child. And Joseph was proving that his promises were all for naught. It was obvious to her that he was not going to stop drinking or blowing all his money. She was right back where she was just one year earlier.

She said that her landlady told Joseph to get lost and to leave poor Elaine alone. And supposedly he got lost. Elaine decided to give the baby to Ethel Cash, the hunchback landlady. A month before she delivered the child, Elaine signed the adoption papers. On September 3, 1945, Elaine had a baby boy at the rooming house.

Ethel Cash let her stay there until Elaine found a place to stay. The boy's name was *Michael James Cash*. Elaine thought she remembered naming him. In any case, Elaine was able to be with the child for a year or so to see the little one grow. Soon, however, the landlady asked her to leave. Elaine said she left, didn't look back, moved to the west side of Cleveland, and started a new life. In less than 15 months, she had given birth to two of Joseph's baby boys and had given them both away. Joseph was nowhere around.

The reason she never told me about the boy, Elaine said, was that she was ashamed of herself for her behavior back then. How could anyone have been so stupid and naive about someone like Joseph, she thought. She accepted the blame though. She didn't have to hook up with him again, she continued. But she did.

When Elaine heard me tell her of the mysterious kid in a coffin, she was shocked. She had no idea that the little one had died, she said. But somehow Joseph found out back in 1951. He had a photo.

At the time of Michael's birth, Elaine was living at 3145 Carnegie Avenue on Cleveland's near east side. Michael was born at 4:30 A.M. on September 3, 1945, and weighed 9¼ lbs. And again, as on my original birth certificate, Joe Homer Baker was listed as "unknown" and white.

## Finding My Brother

Assuming that Joseph was the father of Michael, too, then I had a real full-fledged brother about whom I had just heard. I called my half-sister Norma Nell and told her that I had solved the mystery of the kid in the coffin. As I told her the story, she said she was getting goose bumps. She and I had found out that we had another brother and that our father had had another child.

I wondered when these new doors would stop opening! Just when I thought I had my whole story put together, another door would open. Oh well. I've been there scores of times over the past 30 years chasing Elaine. Let's find Michael.

I called the Cleveland Library and found that his obituary was on microfilm, and that there was an article in the *Cleveland Press* about his death. I called the Catholic diocese and found out that he was buried in southern Cleveland at Calvary Cemetery in Section 77.

That evening, unfortunately after the cemetery offices were closed, I drove to Calvary Cemetery and started roaming Section 77 looking for his grave. But the section where he was buried was a rather large hill covered with thousands of headstones that were flush with the ground and almost all of which were covered with grass clippings and lots of thatch.

After an hour's search, I gave up and decided to come back the next day when the cemetery's office would be open. Maybe they'd give me a diagram of the hill and help me narrow my search.

I took the next day off work, and before I went to the cemetery, drove downtown to the Cleveland library, went into the newspaper room, asked for the November 1951 microfilm, turned on the machine, and . . .

> ***Cleveland Plain Dealer**, November 27, 1951 (p.1), **Widow's Only Child Dies After Running Into Side of Truck**, Michael J. Cash, 6, started home from school for lunch yesterday in that lighthearted mood common to first-graders. But before time for school to take up in the afternoon, he was dead, a victim of traffic hazards that claim the lives of many older than he. Witnesses told police that the boy, who had left Sterling School a few minutes before, ran into the side of a tractor-trailer going north on E. 30th Street at Carnegie Avenue, S.E. The boy was taken to Charity Hospital where he died an hour and a half later. He was the only child of Mrs. Ethel D. Cash, who housed, fed, and clothed the boy and herself by operating a rooming house at 3637 Prospect Avenue S.E. in an old high-ceilinged mansion. Mrs. Cash, a widow, was so upset last night that she could not discuss funeral arrangements. Facts in the case will be presented to the police prosecutor tomorrow. The driver was not held.* [This arti-

cle included a small, grainy outdoor photo of Michael from the waist up]
And,

***Cleveland Press**, November 27, 1951 (p.19),* **Boy, 6, Running Home is City's 96th Auto Victim***, A small boy running home for lunch became Cleveland's 96th traffic fatality. He was Michael Cash, 3637 Prospect Ave., only son of widowed Mrs. Ethel Cash. George Love, 80-year-old school guard was on duty at Carnegie Ave. and E. 30th St., when Michael started home from Sterling School. A chum, James Thacker, 6, of 3205 Carnegie Ave., crossed safely. But Michael ran into the side of a tractor-trailer loaded with steel. He died a short time later in Charity Hospital. The driver told police he saw the boys running but was unable to stop in time, although he said his speed was only 10 to 12 mph.*

Michael's obituary read:
**CASH, MICHAEL JAMES***, residence 3637 Prospect Ave., dearly beloved son of Ethel. Friends may call at Lorree A. Wells Funeral Home, 8806 Euclid Avenue. Services November 29, 10 a.m. from St. Paul's Church, East 40th & Euclid Ave.*

The autopsy report, #70388 M-5010, 3:00 P.M., dated "26$^{th}$ day of November, 1951," which I subsequently got in 1997, stated that there was a post-mortem examination on the body of Michael James Cash of No. 3637 Prospect Avenue, Cleveland, Ohio:

- *Sex: male*
- *Color: white*
- *Age: 6*
- *Weight: 58#*
- *Eyes: Blue*
- *Nativity: American*
- *Complexion: fair*
- *Teeth: fair*
- *Occupation: student*
- *Hair: light brown*
- *Height: 4 ft 0 in*
- *Blood Grouping: type "AB"*

<u>Anatomic Diagnoses</u>
1. *Crushing injury of chest and abdomen*
   a) *Fracture of right $7^{th}$ rib*
   b) *Laceration of right lung, and intra-alveolar hemorrhage, bilateral*
   c) *Hemothorax[16], right*
   d) *Laceration of liver and adrenal*
   e) *Rupture of bladder*
   f) *Hemoperitoneum[17]*

---

[16] *hemothorax*: blood or bloody fluid in the blood vessels resulting from trauma

[17] *hemoperitoneum*: bleeding into the peritoneal cavity

> 2. Multiple contusions, abrasions, and lacerations
>
> ## CAUSE OF DEATH
>
> The decedent came to his death as a result of: crushing injury of chest and abdomen. Tractor-Trailer Accident, Pedestrian. Decedent said to have been struck by a truck while crossing East $30^{th}$ Street at Carnegie Avenue at about 11.51 A.M., 11/26/51. Conveyed to Charity Hospital where he expired at 1.40 P.M., 11.16.1951. (Dr. Smith)

So this was Michael, a full biological brother about whom I didn't know until July of 1996 when I was 52 years old. I had a real brother once. Further research showed that Ethel Cash, the lady who adopted him, had died in 1966. When I contacted Ethel's sister, she told me that Ethel was devastated by the death of Michael whom she adored. Since I knew from the obituary that Michael was buried at Calvary Cemetery, I quickly wrapped up my library visit and, deep in thought, started the long walk back to the lakefront parking lot a few blocks away.

Because of my finding out about Michael, I began to look at Elaine less sympathetically. I could possibly understand her predicament being pregnant with me and being unmarried the first time. I could possibly understand her being charmed by Joseph Homer Baker enough to have a magic moment with him the first time. But to have gone full circle again with my biological father who had already shown himself to be irresponsible and reckless and to have given up another child just 15 months before was too much for me to be understanding or sympathetic. Elaine was not a kid: she was 21 when I was conceived, 22 years old when I was born, and 23 years old when Michael was born.

That morning I brought grass clippers and a whiskbroom for Michael's headstone (just in case it needed sweeping), pencils, and a long roll of wide white paper with which I could do a pencil scratching of the headstone. Since I had also brought my camera, I figured I'd take a few photos of Mike's former home on Prospect Ave. and Sterling Elementary School where he was in the first grade, but Michael's former home on Prospect Avenue was now a parking lot.

I found the Sterling School just a few blocks south and took a photo. A couple blocks north, I took a photo of the intersection at E. 30th and Carnegie where Michael was killed. I knew Norma Nell would be glad to get these little artifacts.

I drove to Calvary Cemetery and went into the main office to find out exactly where Michael's grave was. They gave me a marked-up map, drew a couple arrows on it, and off I went to Section 77, Lot 1893, Grave 2.

I found the section with little trouble since I'd been there the night before, but I couldn't find the gravesite. According to the map, Michael's grave was up a hill in Section 77 near the top. I walked around and around. Nothing. I'd pace a certain number of headstones to the right, just as the map showed, then walk up the hill a certain number of headstones; but I still couldn't find his grave.

"Come on, Mike," I said to myself. "Give me a clue. Rustle a leaf or something, Mike." But he would not give up his secret. I finally went back to the bottom of the hill, studied the headstone map, began walking while meticulously counting each row, and ascended the hill methodically; but I still couldn't find the grave. All I could find was a big bush with long branches low to the ground on the top of the hill right about where Michael's headstone should have been.

Just when I was ready to give up the search, a small gleam of light caught my eye, and something told me (maybe it was Michael's spirit) to lift up one of the bush's branches. And there it was. Under the bush whose branches had spread out over the years, and under a thick growth of grass, thatch, and weeds was the headstone for my dead brother Michael.

> **Michael James Cash**
> Beloved Son
> Sept. 3, 1945 – Nov. 26, 1951

I used my hands to break off the over-hanging branches; my little backyard grass clipper was not up to the task. So I snapped and bent more branches and tore them off. Then I clipped back the overgrown grass surrounding the headstone and brushed off what seemed to be dozens and dozens of years of thatch and leaves. Soon Michael's headstone gleamed at the full sun probably for the first time since his adoptive mother had died way back in 1966.

I made two pencil scratchings of Michael's headstone, one for me and one for my new half-sister Norma Nell. I then gathered all the tools and junk I hauled up to Michael's grave, walked back down the hill, and put everything but the camera back in the car.

I stepped back, took a few pictures of the hill Michael was buried on so Norma could get an idea what the surrounding area looks like, walked up to Michael's grave site, and took a few pictures of the freshly swept headstone. Then, when I was done doing all I was going to do, I put the camera down, knelt there on the sunny hillside at the grave of my dead biological brother, sat back on my heels, clasped my hands, and talked to Michael, the Kid In The Coffin, for the first time:

*Dear Michael,*

*How happy I am to have found out that you're my brother; but how sad it is to find out that you're in a cold, dark coffin six feet under where I'm kneeling. How very sad!*

*But I am your full brother, the son of Elaine Vincent and Joseph Baker, born the year before you were born. I was given up at birth too and raised in Euclid in a house with two other adopted children. I am married to Renee and have three wonderful children, Yvette, Leslie, and Matthew, your nieces and nephew.*

*I am sort of a mild mannered, sensitive person, respectful of other people's property, and keep my children out of other people's yards. I am a conservative kind of guy, extremely Pro-Life, and have returned to God after a few years of doubting and unbelieving. Yeah, I think you would've liked me.*

*I think it's neat that you and I are so close in age. If only Joseph and Elaine had made a decent home for us, we probably would have had lots of fun together.*

*Had you lived, Michael, today we'd be sharing stories of what our kids were doing. And maybe our wives would go shopping together every weekend. And our kids would want to visit Grandma Elaine. And once in a while we'd take our kids to their Grandpa Joe's grave to pay our respects. And we'd be going to ball games and calling each other to talk about how great the Cleveland Indians were doing; after all, you and I would've had season tickets.*

*And I hope that God will be merciful to our mother Elaine for bringing us into the world and giving us up so readily. And may God be merciful to Joseph who with various women had so many children who were then scattered all over.*

*In a couple days, Mike, I'm going to meet one of our half-sisters, Norma Nell, who lives in Huntington, West Virginia. And now that I found out about you, the Baker family will now know exactly who the kid in the coffin was; and now they can keep you in their prayers.*

*And, Michael, that big truck never would've hit you years ago because I, your big brother, would have been firmly holding your grubby little hand as we waited to cross that street. And I hope that when I die and pass to the other side, Michael, you will be there to safely guide me across that boulevard.*

*And I promise to return every so often just to talk to you and to keep that bush away from your headstone.*[18] *No, Michael, you've not been forgotten. But may you rest in peace.*

---

[18] The cemetery workers have since removed the bush after I exposed two other headstones to the right of Michael's.

## Just When I Thought I Was Done Looking...

Needless to say, I was very happy to have successfully found out about Michael and where he was buried; but now I was angry. For the first two years of our reunion, my birth mother Elaine had denied having had any more children; and for two years, I believed her. I thought that we had built a trust and friendship very quickly. But, having had to find out about Michael in the manner which I did was very unsettling to me: my new cousins and new relatives had to tell me about a "kid in a coffin" for a couple months after I found Joe Homer's family in West Virginia before Elaine would admit to something as important as having had another child, my brother.

Of course, I asked Elaine again if she'd had any more children; and, of course, she denied it. The reason she didn't tell me about Michael before, she said, was that she was ashamed of having given away two children in fifteen months. I didn't particularly believe her.

Being the curious guy that I am, on August 26, 1999, I toddled back to downtown Cleveland to the city hall to check the birth registries again—back to the big, clumsy blue books (one for each year) to look for more siblings. Since I was born in 1944, and since Michael was born in September of 1945, I started with the 1946 book.

Each of the registry books back then listed all the "legitimate" births in the front; they were handwritten under each letter of the alphabet. In the back of each of these books was a tabbed section labeled "Illegitimate Births" where the names of the mothers of the illegitimate children had their names listed under each month. In almost all cases, the names on these pages "in the back" were all the female parents' names.

Nothing revealing was in the 1946 book, so on to 1947. And wouldn't you know it, something caught my eye on the October illegitimate page: Joseph Baker/Eunice Hayes. "Oh no!" I said to myself. The only male name on the entire page was Joseph Baker. "Impossible," said I. "Don't tell me that Joe Homer Baker had another child up here in Cleveland, and from a different woman?"

For a quarter, I got a copy of that birth certificate, and lo and behold, there was Joe Baker's name on the father's side of a birth certificate for a *Sally Ann Hayes, born October 18, 1947.* The mother's name was *Eunice F. Buelow.* Sally Ann was listed as Eunice's second child. So, Sally had a sibling from her mother's side other than me from her father's side.

Eunice had listed Joe's correct age and his correct address in Huntington, West Virginia. That was Joe all right! I sat there stunned. I had already found out about Betty Jo, JoAnn, Michael James Cash, Terry Joe, and Norma Nell, which including me, added up to six children of Joe Baker; and now with Sally Ann Hayes added, Joe's progeny count was at seven. Joe's pants had been down again! Somebody should have bought him a belt! Lord Almighty!

So, now my new task, as if I really wanted to go through all this again, was to find Sally Ann Hayes, my newly discovered half-sister. And where would I start? How about at the beginning?

Armed with Sally's 25¢ birth certificate, I walked over to the Cleveland Public Library four or five blocks away to look, yet again, in the city directories to see if I could find any trace of Sally Ann or her mother, Eunice F. Hayes. The 1947 directory showed Eunice living at an address that was listed to a doctor of obstetrics and his family. Searches into the earlier books of the 1940s showed Eunice to have been briefly married to a John Hayes (so that's where she got the name *Hayes)*, and before that, it showed her having lived on Cleveland's east side with her widowed mother and one sister Ruth who later, according to the city directory, became a school teacher.

So, apparently, Eunice was not married to John Hayes around the time that she bumped into —well, more than bumped into—Joe Baker. So, Joe had gotten a newly divorced or widowed young lady pregnant; and somehow his name wound up on Sally Ann's birth certificate and, therefore, on that "illegitimate birth" page. Perhaps Eunice was trying to get Joe Baker to pay child support. Since she didn't give Sally Ann Joe's last name, I could only surmise that Eunice wanted to make it clear on the birth certificate and in the official record as to whom Sally's father was.

But where was Sally Ann? Did Eunice keep Sally? Did she give her up? Subsequent searches of later city directories turned up neither Sally Ann nor Eunice Hayes. Where did everybody go?

A trip to the city hall to dig through the divorce records was in order. And, yes, I found on their divorce decree that Eunice and John Hayes had gotten divorced a year or so before Sally's birth. And the decree mentioned that Eunice was to get full custody of a little girl named Linda, who would therefore be Sally Ann's older half sister.

Since I couldn't find anything on Sally and Eunice, I thought I'd see if Linda could be traced. The only thing that might have her name on it would probably be a marriage license. As luck would have it, I found a marriage license for a Linda Hayes who would have been about the correct age according to the divorce decree. And therefore, Linda's new husband's name, Thomas, was listed too. How about looking in the Cleveland phone book to see if Linda's husband was listed. What luck! He was listed (or at least someone with that same name). So, I picked up the phone and called the number that was listed for him and struck oil.

After all these years, Linda was still married to Tom; and, yes, she knew about her mother having had another child while not married. But that was all she knew except that Eunice's second child was rumored to be a girl. Linda had been put into an orphanage on Cleveland's west side since her mother was having personal problems. Linda stayed there throughout her childhood and adolescence and then married and, fortunately for me in my search, stayed married to the same man.

But where and who was Sally? The city hall adoption record departments would not lift a finger to help me. They would neither deny nor confirm having any adoption folder for Sally Ann since all adoption records were sealed.

I called *USSEARCH* after hearing them brag after a *Montel Williams* show that "we can find anybody." Sounded good to me!

"What information do you have on her?" they asked.

"Well," I told them, "all I have is her birth certificate."

"Was she adopted?"

"I have no idea. She seems to disappear as soon as she is born."

"Well," they said. "You don't have enough information for us to help you. If you knew if she was adopted, we could help you."

"Believe me," I answered. "If I knew the answer to that, I would have already found her." And I said that with confidence.

Internet searches didn't help because there were scores and scores of Sally Hayeses around the country. And, of course, if she'd gotten married, her name wouldn't be Hayes anyway. So, basically, my search for my geographically closest sibling had ground to a halt.

But, I had been grounded to a halt numerous times before, hadn't I? What to do? I got into numerous adoption web sites on the Internet and posted messages here and there about trying to find Sally Ann

Hayes. No one responded. So, I put all my documents in one big office envelope, the kind with the holes and string tie, put it in a drawer, and tried to figure out what to do next.

Four years after I started looking for Sally, I got an email from a lady south of Cleveland who asked me how my search had gone. She had run across my name on a message I had left on one of those Internet adoption sites. I emailed her that I had stopped looking and really didn't know where to go next.

She offered to help if she could. She had helped other adoptees find missing relatives and would be glad to see what she could do. Armed only with Sally Ann's birth date and knowing that Sally was born here in Cleveland on October 18, 1947, she went through a database or two that had the names of people applying for credit or other things where they had to list where and when they were born.

Somehow, she came up with two possible names of people who just might be good prospects. And in a couple days she emailed me giving me two names and addresses of likely candidates. Still a bit discouraged about trying to find Sally Ann, I got to my keyboard and wrote a small note to the first name in the email.

I let the addressee know that I was looking for a Sally Ann Hayes who was born October 18, 1947, and whose mother's name was Eunice Frances Hayes. I mentioned in my letter that Sally and I had the same father, Joseph Homer Baker, who was born in Huntington, West Virginia. The note was not long, but it was specific. Then I toddled down to the nearest mailbox and dropped it in.

On May 22, 2003, the very next day, after I had just returned from work, the phone rang.

"Are you Larry Weeks?" a man's voice asked.

"Yes," I answered, thinking that this is a salesman.

"Are you the one looking for Sally Ann Hayes?" he continued.

I froze. "Yes."

"Well, Sally is my wife, and she's sitting on the couch right now and is too nervous to talk to you. Her name now is Barbara."

I couldn't believe it. After over four years of searching, I found another scattered sibling. This was too good to be true. After a few minutes of us trading information over the phone to confirm that we were who we said we were, he said, "Barb's ready to talk to you now."

"Larry? This is Barb," said the new voice. She began to tell me a story that a Cleveland-area family adopted her at birth, and her first name was immediately changed to Barbara. A nice family raised both her and a boy that they had likewise adopted. "I've had a good life," she said. "I now live in Hudson, Ohio." The city of Hudson is about a 45-minute ride from my house in Mentor.

Barb said she had her original birth certificate before her name change (a copy of the same birth certificate that I already had) and, therefore, always knew that she had an older sibling since it was mentioned on the document that she was the second child of her mother.

"That's not I, Barb. You have an older sister named Linda who lives in Solon, about ten miles from you. You and Linda had the same mother; you and I have the same father." And I told her that she had quite a large family of half-sisters and half-brothers scattered all over the country.

We arranged to meet at noon at *Fridays* restaurant in Mayfield Heights, which was about half way between both our homes.

"How will I know who you are?" Barb asked.

"I'll be sitting near the front door and will have a large yellow inter-office envelope with me, the kind that have holes in them. How will I know who you are?" I asked.

"I'm kinda' short, have straight blond hair, and my husband is a big guy. We'll be there at noon."

I quickly telephoned her half-sister Linda in Solon. I hadn't talked to Linda in a few years since I ran into the Sally Ann Hayes information drought. Linda was ecstatic about the news of my having found her half-sister, and I asked her to walk in on us at 1 p.m., an hour later, that same Saturday.

When Saturday came, I sat at a table near the front door, put my large yellow inter-office envelope prominently in front of me on the table, and waited. At noon, in walked a short lady with straight blond hair accompanied by a bigger fellow who had a camera hanging around his neck. It was Barb and her husband Jack.

Barbara was thrilled to meet me and just sat there staring at me. I didn't know if she heard half of what I was saying, but she seemed so happy. She and her husband had looked for years for the "older sibling" on her birth certificate and eventually gave up.

Earlier that week, her husband said he watched while she opened the letter I sent her. She read it for a few moments, and then exclaimed, "Oh my God, Jack!" While staring into space, Jack said she turned white. "Read this," she said, handing the letter to Jack. He thought that maybe it was a bill or something, but then was likewise shocked after reading my little missive.

We talked and talked, and showed each other photos from over the years from each of our lives. I was pleased and felt again that I had done something very nice for a couple people. The time flew by; and, just as it got to be 1 p.m., in walked Linda and her husband. I didn't tell Barb that I had this other surprise for her. I hadn't met her half-sister Linda either and had only talked to her once in a while during the past four years of my search. But I spotted them easily because Linda's husband likewise had a camera hung around his neck and somehow they instinctively knew what was going on at our table. They instantly came over.

"Barb," I said as my voice started to tremble, "I'd like you to meet your older sister Linda." Barb had the most shocked look on her face. She was stunned. For the next couple hours, the five of us exchanged pleasantries and volumes of snippets from each of our lives. Barb sat between Linda and me just turning her head back and forth, back and forth, looking at Linda and then back to me. And a photo that Linda had brought of Eunice, their mother, showed that Barbara was a spitting image of her—absolutely identical. This reunion could not have been scripted any better. This was a once-in-a-lifetime experience for everybody at our table. Hey, Maury, Montel, and Oprah! We don't need you!!

## THOUGHTS

My wife, whose former husband abandoned her shortly after her daughter Leslie was born, had her doubts about whether or not she could accept the friendship of my birthmother Elaine who gave up her two children some 50 odd years ago. How could anyone do that, my wife repeated. I couldn't answer. How could a mother who had carried a baby actually give it away? I had the privilege of watching my wife be a good mother to our children, and I guess she had a very good point. And I fought for and won the custody of my child from a previous marriage because I couldn't for a minute bear to not see my child on a daily basis. Little Yvette was my flesh and blood.

Times were different in the 40s and 50s when I grew up in Euclid, Ohio. What were you to think of a woman who had a child and who wasn't married? On our block, there were no such people. Almost all the mothers were home taking care of their children and making sure the houses were in order for their families.

There were no daycare centers; they just didn't exist. The moms were at home taking care of the children most certainly until the youngest child was old enough to go to school. Those days are now long gone. Even kindergarten was looked upon then as a place that a mom of lesser "motherliness" would put her preschool children. I remember my adoptive mother saying that kindergarten was nothing more than a baby sitter.

But most certainly, there were "unwed" moms. If fate had made the mother a widow, the community chipped in and helped. There were no agencies or high-minded social workers in some distant concrete office judging what was best for the widow and her children. The local moms and dads chipped in; or at the very least, the local church was notified of the widow's distress, and the community helped her.

One has to return to the 40s and 50s to understand that in those years (probably the last of the years) an unwed mother was looked down upon. In our so-called new and modern day and age, we look upon the 40s and 50s as being archaic and too judgmental. The mere fact that it was shameful to be pregnant *and* unmarried was enough to limit—very severely limit—unwed births. There were few abortions as a way out. There was difficulty finding an excuse to hide anywhere while you had your "illegitimate" child. And, if you decided to keep the child, you were branded instantly as a loose woman. Fair or unfair, society was different back then.

* * *

In February of 2004, Elaine died of complications of cancer. Elaine and I had known each other personally for almost ten years. Our reunion was very rewarding for both of us. She met my wife and my three children and reveled in the attention, visits, and phone calls that she never would have gotten had she decided not to go through with this reunion.

Our first Christmas was unique for each of us. I personally don't like to go anywhere for Christmas. I'd rather stay home and watch the wife and kids open their gifts, and just relax. Well, that first Christmas for Elaine and me was special. I told the family that just this once, only this one time, I promised, let's all go and give Elaine her first Christmas with her son and his family.

Everyone agreed; and on Christmas morning almost a month to the day of our 50-year reunion, we made the forty-mile journey to the other side of Cleveland and exchanged gifts with Elaine. My family took to her quickly and was instantly charmed by Elaine's happy and light-hearted nature. The twinkle in her deep blue eyes and her constant kidding around won their hearts.

We opened gifts, hugged, talked, and laughed. It was a grand Christmas. I had a feeling that it meant more—much more—to Elaine. Certainly, I was happy. I felt that I had done a wonderful thing for someone, probably much more wonderful than I really knew.

For quite a few years, Elaine and I went for many car rides. I took her to the neighborhood where I was raised, showed her the house in which I lived as a child, the park I played in, and the schools that I attended in Euclid. I drove her to the golf course where I was a caddie for four years and showed her the various places where I grew up and spent my childhood.

One day I drove her to Parmadale, the west side Catholic campus that used to be an orphanage. Nowadays the complex is used to house run-away, problem, and abused children. I wanted to show Elaine where I would have been had I not been adopted. The campus is very serene and well kept. I would have been in good hands with the dear nuns, I assured her.

When possible we visited the cemetery where Elaine's husband was buried back in 1972. Sometimes I would stop there before I picked her up so I could plant a flower or two at his grave. She enjoyed the surprise; and since she couldn't get around too easily, I wanted to help her do a few things that she couldn't otherwise do.

I called her almost every other day and visited her almost every other week. Elaine would await my calls and would remind me if I forgot to call once in a while. But since I looked forward to calling her, it didn't happen too often. And as long as the good Lord allowed us to know each other, I looked forward to many years of Elaine's company.

## THE SCATTERED SIBLINGS

As the next years unfolded, I found half-siblings and had many unions (or "reunions") with my newly discovered relatives. In the order of their birth, here's a summary of the siblings involved in this story:

- **Betty Jo Baker, my oldest half-sister**: Betty Jo was Joe Baker's oldest child, born of his first marriage. Following the divorce of Joe Baker and her mother, Betty Jo was raised by her mother and put in various private schools.

  In 1951, while going to Andrews Girls Academy in Willoughby, Ohio, she got a call from her grandmother who told Betty that she was up in Cleveland attending the funeral of a neighbor boy of Betty's Aunt Freda who lived in Euclid. The little boy had been run over by a truck. Betty said it seemed odd that her grandmother would drive all the way to Cleveland to attend the funeral of a non-related neighbor of her aunt. Betty was shocked to find out from me that the funeral was for Michel Cash, her half-brother that Joe Baker had up in Cleveland.

  Betty died a few years ago with complications from diabetes.

- **JoAnn Baker, my second older half-sister**: JoAnn was Joe Baker's second child. Joe was married to JoAnn's mother when my mother Elaine claims to have found out that Joe was already married and had a child. JoAnn's mother never had anything good to say about Joe Baker or the

Baker family, which is probably why JoAnn was and still is very cool to re-uniting with Norma and me.

JoAnn lived in Florida and was involved in real estate. She recently moved back to Huntington, West Virginia.

- **I, Lawrence Andrew Weeks (aka Joseph Allan Vincent)**: I turned 68 in 2012. I have a bachelor's degree with a major history from Cleveland State University. My discovery of another half-sibling, Sally Ann Hayes, convinced me to stop looking; it seems that Joe Baker was a bit prolific and indiscriminate in his meanderings. Besides, Lord knows what I'll find. I love Civil War history; and, if I were king, I'd like to spend the rest of my life writing non-fiction and digging through battlefields.

  I am presently a business skills instructor at a private vocational school in Mentor, Ohio, am married to Reneé, and have three children:

- **Yvette** (from my first marriage) lives in Green Bay. She's the young lady who wanted to go up to Elaine's trailer to knock on her door. Yvette has a bachelor's degree in anthropology from Cleveland State, is married to Frank, and has two sons, Antonio who is 9 years old and Roman who is 8 years old.

- **Leslie** (from my wife's first marriage, whom I adopted) has a master's degree in occupational therapy from University of Indianapolis. She is married to Curt Hunnewell, and has two children:

a two year old daughter Aida whom she adopted from Moscow in 2011, and a natural born son Paxton who is one year old. When Leslie and Curt went before the Moscow judge to talk about why they wanted to adopt Aida, Leslie said that her father (I) was adopted, and that I adopted her, and that she'd like to adopt Aida to keep that string going. And I guess the judge agreed.

- **Matthew**, Reneé's and my child from this marriage, is a practicing attorney along with his wife Jennifer. They have a 16 year old son Anthony.
- **Michael James Cash, my full brother**: At this writing, I still have not found the picture of "the boy in the coffin." No one seems to know where the photo is, but I will continue to look for it. The bush over Michael's grave has since been removed, so not only his grave but also two more headstones from other burials in 1951 are now visible.

Interestingly, Michael died on November 26, 1951; and my first visit to Elaine was 43 years later on the same date, November 26, 1994. Also, my closest friend Ray whom I've known since my early teen years has his birthday on November 26.

Many was the time I'd bring Elaine to the cemetery, put her in her wheelchair, and pull her backwards up the hill to Michael's grave. Then I'd leave her to her thoughts.

A few years ago, I planted crocus and tulip bulbs around Michael's headstone and then planted the same kind around the tree in my front yard

25 miles away in Mentor, Ohio. This way, when I see that the bulbs are blooming at my home, I know that they're blooming at Michael's grave, too.

- **Barbara (Sally) Ann Hayes, my half-sister:** Barbara and I keep in touch. Since she lives so close to her new half-sister Linda, they've become best of friends and go many places together.
- **Terry Joe Baker, my half-brother:** Terry was the first half-sibling who contacted me after my trip to Huntington. Terry had numerous health and emotional problems throughout his life involving drugs, gambling, domestic violence, and alcohol. He married only once, and that was for only a year.

  Terry had musical talent and wrote numerous songs, three of which he had recorded. He and I met occasionally whenever I visited Norma. He never had any children. Claiming illness from chemical exposure in the service, he lived his last few years on governmental disability. Terry, a heavy cigarette smoker, was found dead in his apartment November 22, 2002, after bouts with emphysema and asthma.

  When Terry died, Norma Nell kept his cremated ashes in an urn to await my next trip to Huntington. She wanted me to go with her to the Sixth Street Bridge (State Highway 527) over the Ohio River that connects Huntington and Chesapeake to dispose of Terry's ashes per his request. We're not supposed to do that, said Norma, because the

EPA has decided that it pollutes the river. Well, we broke the law.

On my next trip to Huntington, about nine months after his death, we pulled into a *Bob Evans* restaurant at the foot of the Huntington side of the bridge. Norma had the box with the urn in a gym bag. She popped open the trunk of the car, lifted the bag out, and handed it to me to carry. "These are heavier than I thought they'd be," I said to Norma while pointing to the bag. I had never handled human cremation remains before. "Oh, I'll carry them for you," said Norma. I looked her in the eye and said, "He's not heavy—he's my brother." Norma burst out laughing. "If Terry were here he'd be laughing," said Norma. "He IS here," I said, pointing to the bag. Now, we both were laughing—nothing like a little black humor.

When we got to the top of the bridge, we sat down against the back of a walkway, dangled our legs over the side, and began to get ready for Terry's last journey. I used my pocketknife to open the top of the plastic container that held Terry's ashes. Inside the container was a plastic bag with a twist-tie at the top.

I lifted the bag out of the container and started to untwist the tie. "No, no," said Norma. "Let's poke a hole in the bottom of the bag instead, and let the ashes go out slowly." "Poke it with what?" I asked. "Use your pocketknife."

So, I lifted the bag with Terry's ashes, reopened my pocketknife, and shoved the point into the bottom of the bag. "Oh, my God," I said to Norma. "I just stabbed our brother." Catching on to the sick humor, Norma immediately said, "Yeah, and now we're going to throw him off a bridge."

While we began to laugh at our dark humor, I held the bag out over the edge of the bridge, took away my hand, and instead of slowly coming out of the bag, the ashes shot through the bottom like they were blown out of a cannon. A huge white cloud of Terry's remains blew out over the river.

About a hundred yards or so down the Ohio River was an open fishing boat. Just as the ash cloud roared out of the bag, the fisherman in the open boat looked up at the top of the bridge and clearly saw what was coming toward him.

Terry's ashes floated right for his boat. "Well, Norma," I said, "Terry's gon' a' fishin' today." "The guy in the fishing boat won't know what the white cloud is, will he?" asked Norma. "Well, what do you think he'll think the white cloud is, vacuum cleaner ashes? Of course he'll know what they are. Let's get out of here."

Some of the ashes landed on a few of the bridge's beams. I assured Norma that God would take care of those ashes during the next rain. Each of us had a little of Terry's residue on our clothes, so when we had lunch in *Bob Evans* following our informal ceremony, Terry went to lunch with us too.

Norma took the remaining crumbs of his ashes that were in the plastic bag and buried them on Memorial Day 2005 between their mother's and father's headstones on a quiet hill in Alkol, West Virginia.

- **Norma Nell Baker, my half-sister**: Norma was the first half-sibling I personally met back in 1996 when she and her husband Lyle drove up to Cambridge, Ohio, half way between her home and mine. We decided to meet at a *Cracker Barrel* restaurant in Cambridge. Norma and her husband drove up from Alkol, West Virginia; and I drove down from Mentor, Ohio. I got to the restaurant just moments before they did.

    Already knowing that they'd appear in a red jeep, I saw them pull in and stop just as I sat down in a rocking chair outside the restaurant. Norma got out of the jeep, looked at me sitting in the rocking chair, and rushed forward with her arms out. "Larry!" she yelled as she ran up and hugged me as I began to stand up. "Lady," I said as she hugged me, "I'm just here to fix the air conditioning!" She stepped back startled, looked at me, saw me laughing; and we then hugged even harder.

    We hit if off quickly, and soon we were swapping visits every year to each other's homes. Norma has three children: two boys and a girl. Today, Norma and Lyle are raising her grandson

Corey, who is from a broken home, and are giving the young man a great chance to grow up in a loving environment.

## Other Principals In This Story

- **Elaine Marie Vincent:** My birth mother was an interesting but private woman. Although I was thrilled to have met her after all those years of searching, once I found out about little Michael and how she'd had two children in 15 months and had given up both of them, I began to have a less positive view of her and her behavior. Family rumors from Ethyl Cash's sister, the hunch-back lady to whom Elaine gave little Michael, suggested that Elaine had actually sold the little guy to Ethyl for two or three hundred dollars, a deal made well before the little guy's birth.

  In Elaine's favor is the fact that around 1951, around the time that Michael got killed, she moved to the west side of Cleveland, got away from Joe Baker, got a room with a family, and got a respectable job. This respectability belied her past so well that even a close social friend such as the lady at Langenau Mfg. who first told me about Elaine, was shocked to find out that Elaine had had an illegitimate child. Throughout the remainder of Elaine's life, I continued to wonder what other secrets she was not sharing with me.

  And I never saw Elaine make even a feeble attempt to right herself with the God that she had grown up with as a child. I offered to take her to church a number of times, but she always refused.

  The time I spent with her riding through parks or sitting around watching TV in her trailer was generally pleasant although she'd frequently become very critical of her nephew-in-law Lester who had been living with her and helping her do daily things for quite a few years. She seldom finished a sentence without injecting some kind of joke into the meaning. And she loved her Cleveland Browns and Cleveland Indians.

As mentioned before, Elaine died in February of 2004 and is buried next to her only husband (and perhaps her only love), James E. Lewis, in Olmsted Falls, Ohio.

**Homer (Joseph) Baker:** I never got to meet Joe Homer (or Homer Joe) since he died in 1990. I'm not sure what he would of thought of me if I had met him before he died. Apparently, he never had too many serious moments in his life. Everyone seemed to like him.

But everyone said his drinking overshadowed his good nature. His brother Thomas said that he'd occasionally get Joe Homer surveying jobs on the various highway projects around Huntington. But once Joe put together a bankroll, the temptation to hit the bottle was too strong.

My cousins Larry and Debbie said that Joe was always a meticulous dresser and quite the ladies man. Although he might not have a pot to put anything in, Joe always seemed to have shined shoes, a dapper suit, snazzy tie, and all the other accoutrements.

Norma Nell, Joe's youngest child, said that he would have been very proud of me. Since Terry

Joe was such a disappointment in his and everybody else's eyes, he would have been proud of me, his first son. But Cousin Larry said that he doubted if Joe would have been any more than mildly impressed. I, in my own self-righteous way, feel that I would have been fascinated to meet him, my biological father, but that I think that I would also have been repelled by his attitude toward his women, children (my siblings), and life itself.

Supposedly, according to Cousin Larry, Joe went through a variety of jobs up here in Cleveland. On one of these jobs, Joe Homer was a bus driver in one of those old electrical buses that had antennas reaching up to an electrical screen that covered some streets. Well, Joe wasn't too happy working one day, rounded the corner with his bus at a high rate of speed, turned his bus out from under the electrical grid, and coasted into the parking lot of a saloon nearby. With the change from his bus, he went into the bar and drank it all away. Another time, Joe was supposed to have driven his beer truck into a park where a buddy of his who drove a bread truck met him, and the two guys drank and ate to their hearts' content.

On one of my trips to visit Cousin Larry and Debby, they drove me to a small building in Chesapeake, Ohio, that was basically a drunk tank: couple rooms, bars on the window, and probably a potty.

More than once, Larry said he'd be driving past the drunk tank, and he'd see Joe's smiling face peeking out while waving his hand. Larry would then cross the Ohio River, get bail money from Joe's mother, drive back to Chesapeake, bail Joe out, and drive Joe home. Otis Campbell of Mayberry, meet Joe Homer of Chesapeake.

I asked Norma if Joe had ever really had a serious moment, something that he might have shared with her, some thoughts, perhaps, about how he'd screwed up his life and could have done so much more if only he'd have been more mature and responsible. "No," she answered. The only artifact that Norma could find of Joe's to give me as a memento was a small coffee cup that she said was his favorite.

But, alas, Norma said that Joe seldom showed emotion; and even when he was in the hospital for his last few days on earth, knowing that he was soon going to die, he never took anyone aside to confide with or to bare his soul. Norma did, however, see him once in his final few days with tears in his eyes. But he didn't tell her why.

- **My adoptive Mother, Caroline Weeks:** My adoptive mother died at the age of 99 in August of 2006, and lived in the same house on Ball Avenue where I was raised with my sister Madonna. When she was alive, I used to visit her once a week so my sister could go out and do shopping or whatever, just so my adoptive mother didn't get in any trouble or get hurt. She was quite weak and had little short-term memory.

My adoptive mother and I never did reconcile our lifelong problems, but, life goes on.

- **My younger adoptive sister, Madonna***:* She learned a few years after I found out about my biological family and was not too thrilled. Even though I could probably find her roots too, Donna said she'd just rather not know. I have in my possession her original birth certificate under her birth name just in case she changes her mind.
- **My older adoptive brother, Michael**: Mike expressed interest in a search for his biological family a few years ago after he learned that I had found my biological roots. After a very brief search, I found that he had two half-sisters in Western Pennsylvania. His biological mother had passed away in the early 90s in Fremont, Ohio; and it's still unclear as to who his father was because there's virtually no one alive who would know. Mike got to meet both his half-sisters shortly after I found out where they lived.
- **Baby Boy Weeks, the stillborn baby my adoptive mother had**: On one of Norma Nell's trips to Cleveland, she and I went to Calvary Cemetery where I found out that "Baby Boy Weeks," the stillborn baby that my adoptive parents had, who would've been my age, had been buried in a special section reserved for stillborn and infant deaths.

So, three of the principals in this story are buried there: Michael James Cash, my biological brother; Ethyl Cash, the woman to whom Elaine gave (or sold) Michael when he was born; and the little stillborn baby my adoptive parents had in 1944. Norma and I couldn't find a marker for the stillborn baby although we had a section map. So, we had to approximate the baby's grave's location in relation to where we found other graves that had markers.

Apparently, there was a lot less ceremonial burial activity for stillborns back in the 1940s. A local funeral home associate told me that back then a stillbirth was not something that people talked about. It was considered more of an event not worthy of much discussion or ceremony, almost as if it was a personal failure; and things were taken care of quietly and discreetly.

- **Dr. Larry and Debbie Baker**: In the late summer of 2004, I had the privilege of meeting two more of my cousins, Larry and Debbie, who had just returned from a couple years of missionary work in India. Although I had spoken to them back in 1996, I had never met them in person. Doctor Larry opened a practice in Charleston, West Virginia, after he moved back to be near his parents.

Interestingly, I am a first child, second child, and a third child, depending on which biological family unit you look at: I am my biological mother's first child. I am my adoptive parents' second child, Michael being the first child; and I am the third child of Joseph Homer Baker, third after Betty Jo Baker and then Jo-Ann Baker.

I'm sure that I will find out more and more as time goes by, but I've decided to end this story now. Norma Nell and I still swap phone calls, visits, and photos. I knew I was going to enjoy the first meeting with a Baker back in 1996. After all, I got my first impression of them through my half-sister Norma Nell. During our first phone call in 1996, I asked Norma Nell what she would like me to call her: Norma Nell, Norma, Nell, or Nellie. Without missing a beat, and in the most adorable West Virginia accent, she said, "Just call me Sis."

And then I can't forget what my new half-sister Barbara in Hudson, Ohio, told me after I found her up here in northern Ohio: "You've changed my life." Now that's a very happy ending to a very long story.

**About the Author**

The author, Lawrence A. Weeks, was born in Cleveland, Ohio, and was given up at birth to be adopted. Just before he was two years old, he was adopted by a family in Euclid, Ohio, where his adopted mother and adopted sister lived. Despite being told that his parents died in a car crash after he was just born, Mr. Weeks embarked on a rather long search to find out things that most people take for granted: birth certificate, birth parents, birth siblings, etc. He graduated from Euclid High School and then got a Bachelor's Degree from Cleveland State with a major in history.

He now lives in Mentor, Ohio, with his wife of over 35 years. Mr. Weeks is a business skills instructor at a medical-vocational school near his home. He has been a speaker with the Greater Cleveland Right To Life and has done volunteer work at his local chapter. His oldest daughter, Yvette, the one whose birth initiated his long search, is married to Frank, lives in Green Bay and has two children, Anthony and Roman. His youngest daughter, Leslie, is an Occupation Therapist, married to Curt and has two children, Aida (adopted from Russia) and their natural child Paxton, and his son, Matthew, a lawyer, who is married to Jennifer (also a lawyer), and has a stepson Anthony.

Made in the USA
Las Vegas, NV
14 September 2021

# Still His Mama

By Terrell Hatzilias, PhD

Copyright © 2024 Terrell Hatzilias

All rights reserved. In accordance with U.S. Copyright Act of 1976, the scanning, uploading, and electronic sharing of any part of this book without permission of the publisher constitute unlawful piracy and theft of the author's intellectual property. No part of this book may be reproduced in any form by any electronic or mechanical means (including photocopying, recording or information storage and retrieval) without permission in writing from the author or publisher. Thank you for your support of the author's rights. For bulk or wholesale orders, please contact us admin@richterpublishing.com.

Book Cover Design: By Richter Publishing LLC, photo taken by Olga Kurat, Kegan's shadow image added by Sarah Henderson (from Saying Goodbye, a division of the Mariposa Trust).

Editors: Julia Florey, Austin Hatch & Abigail Bunner

Publisher: Richter Publishing LLC www.richterpublishing.com

ISBN-13: 978-1-954094-45-1 Paperback